WILLIAM F. HALSEY:
Fighting Admiral

Admiral William F. Halsey, Jr., usually managed to be where the fighting was. *Attack repeat Attack* was his motto and a familiar message signaled from his flagship. His story is largely the story of the sea war in the Pacific during World War II as the U. S. Navy fought its way back from defeat at Pearl Harbor to victory over the Japanese. But Halsey was not only one of the most aggressive fighting admirals of all time; author Chandler Whipple also reveals him as a warm, kindly man who became one of America's most beloved leaders.

LIVES TO

REMEMBER

William F. Halsey:

Fighting Admiral

by CHANDLER WHIPPLE

G. P. PUTNAM'S SONS  NEW YORK

© 1968 by Chandler Whipple
All rights reserved
Published simultaneously in the Dominion
of Canada by Longmans Canada Limited, Toronto
Library of Congress Catalog Card Number: 67–24180
PRINTED IN THE UNITED STATES OF
AMERICA
12216

Contents

ACKNOWLEDGMENTS

First, I wish to thank Mrs. Reynolds Wilson (Admiral Halsey's sister Deborah), who, with typical Halsey courtesy, graciously gave me her time and some choice reminiscences concerning her brother, as did the Admiral's cousin, Henry Bayard Clark. Admiral Robert B. Carney, USN (Ret.) was also kind enough to provide me with a great deal of Halsey material. Special thanks should likewise go to Rear Admiral Ernest M. Eller, USN (Ret.), director of the Naval History Division of the Navy Department, and his executive officer, Rear Admiral F. Kent Loomis, USN (Ret.). Were there room to do so, I should like to name each member of the staff of Naval History, both in the Library and the Navy Yard Annex, for it seems to me that they labored beyond the call of duty to open for me the extensive files of Halsey papers collected by Commander W. G. Neville, Jr., USNR, which included not only war diaries, action reports, and clippings, but a vast amount of Halsey correspondence as well. The National Archives also provided me with ships' logs for 1918 of the U.S.S. *Benham* and the U.S.S. *Shaw*, as well as other naval files concerning Halsey. Vice Admiral John F. Shafroth, USN (Ret.) and Rear Admiral J. F. Greenslade, USN (Ret.) of the Naval Historical Foundation were likewise helpful to me, as were Mrs. G. Bertram Woodruff and the Pingry School.

Thanks also go to Rear Admiral Samuel Eliot Morison, USNR (Ret.) for permission to use the quotation from his *The Two-Ocean War* (Little, Brown, & Co., 1963); to the Chilton

8

Company for the two Burke quotations from *Admiral Arleigh (31-Knot) Burke*, by Ken Jones and Hubert Kelley, Jr. (Chilton Books, 1962); and to Simon & Schuster for the Halsey quotation from *Words to Live By*, edited by William Nichols and copyrighted 1947 by United Newspapers Magazine Corporation (Simon & Schuster, 1947).

All quotations followed by an asterisk are from *Admiral Halsey's Story*, by Fleet Admiral William F. Halsey, USN, and J. Bryan III, published by Whittlesey House, McGraw-Hill Book Company, Inc.; copyright, 1947, by William F. Halsey; copyright, 1947, by The Curtis Publishing Company; and reprinted by permission of Brandt & Brandt.

In addition, the following publications were consulted:

History of United States Naval Operations in World War II, Vols. IV, V, VI, VII, VIII, XII and XV, by Samuel Eliot Morison (Little, Brown & Co., 1949-1960).

The Great Sea War, edited by E. B. Potter and Fleet Admiral Chester W. Nimitz, USN (Prentice-Hall, Inc., 1960).

Fleet Admiral King, by Fleet Admiral Ernest J. King, USN and W. M. Whitehill (Norton, 1952).

Midway, The Battle That Doomed Japan, by Mitsuo Fuchida and Masatake Okumiya (U. S. Naval Institute, 1955).

Coral and Brass, by General Holland M. Smith, USMC (Ret.) and Percy Finch (Scribner's, 1949).

Battle Report, Vol. I, by Commander Walter Karig, USNR, and Lieutenant Welbourn Kelley, USNR (Farrar & Rinehart, Inc., 1944).

Thirty Seconds over Tokyo, by Captain Ted W. Lawson, USAAF (Random House, 1943).

The Sea and the States, by Samuel W. Bryant (Thomas Y. Crowell Co., 1947).

Our Many-Sided Navy, by Robert Wilden Neeser (Yale University Press, 1914).

The Bluejackets' Manual (U. S. Naval Institute, 1944).

United States Naval Chronology, World War II (Naval History Division, Navy Department, 1955).

U. S. Strategic Bombing Survey (Pacific) (Government Printing Office, 1946).

Aviation in the United States Navy, 1961 and *Destroyers in the United States Navy, 1962* (Naval History Division, Government Printing Office).

Halsey's Famous Signals, by R. H. Roupe (U. S. Naval Institute Proceedings, August, 1951).

Where Is Task Force Thirty-four?, by Andrew Hamilton (U. S. Naval Institute Proceedings, October, 1960).

Bull's Run, by Gilbert Cant (*Life* Magazine, November 24, 1947).

Newsweek, October 29, 1945.

Various newspapers, including the Wellington, New Zealand *Dominion,* the Minneapolis *Morning Tribune,* the New York *Times,* the Richmond *Times-Despatch,* and the Washington *Times-Herald.*

C.W.

WILLIAM F. HALSEY:
Fighting Admiral

1. A LETTER TO THE PRESIDENT

ON A CRISP DAY in November 1945 the city of Elizabeth, New Jersey, turned out to honor its hero, Fleet Admiral William F. Halsey, Jr. This was the home-town boy whose genius and daring had helped so greatly to bring the war in the Pacific to a victorious end. Bands blared and thousands of cheering citizens lined the streets. Newspapers headlines flared, and the inside pages were filled with accounts of his deeds.

After the parade a smaller group met to hold another ceremony. The town placed a plaque upon the house where he had been born 63 years earlier. A boyhood friend and schoolmate stood beside the Admiral, watching the proceedings with amusement.

"Instead of putting up that thing saying Admiral Halsey was born here," he said, "they ought to put up a statue that says, 'Bull Halsey fought here.' "

Halsey's familiar smile lit up his rugged face. "Bart

Woodruff," he said in his gentle voice, "you go to blazes."

In the memory of boyhood friends like Lieutenant Colonel G. Bertram Woodruff, Willie Halsey had always been a fighter. But that nickname "Bull" had been fastened on him by mistake during the war. Apparently a newspaperman in the Pacific, typing out a story in a hurry, had written "Bull" instead of "Bill," and the name had stuck because back in the States everyone thought it fit him. He was in fact normally a soft-spoken, gentle-mannered man, sometimes profane and picturesque in speech, but always able to laugh at himself, no matter how great he became. To his friends he had been "Willie," then "Pudge," and finally "Bill." He did not care much for this new name, but in time he came to accept it with wry good humor.

This was now a different Elizabeth from the one where he had been born on October 30, 1882. It had been only a small city then, of thirty-odd thousand people, with wide, tree-shaded streets, and many old homes that dated back to the American Revolution. Now it was a bustling, commercial city three times larger, practically a suburb of New York, and without much room for shade trees.

Other things had changed too. Life was more hurried and more crowded now. By comparison, its pace had been very slow in those days. The automobile, the airplane, radio and television did not exist, and families had to provide a great deal of their own entertainment. To homes in the city, ice came in big chunks brought by a horse-drawn cart, and you put the chunk in your icebox to keep food from spoiling. In fact, most of the things you ate and wore were brought by train or horse-drawn vehicle or bicycle. Coal or wood provided the power for steamships, and there were still plenty of sailing vessels. Ladies wore voluminous long skirts which swept the muddy or dusty streets that would not be paved for years to come.

It was a comfortable world Willie Halsey came into on that October day, but a rather strange one too, for it seemed to be ruled over by his beautiful and adoring mother. He knew that he also had a father, but the picture he built of him was vague. He supposed he must be an important man, for he was an officer of the United States Navy, now somewhere far away at sea.

Willie, still wearing the long yellow curls of which his mother was so proud, was two and a half years old when the word arrived that his father was coming home. His ship would dock in New York that afternoon. His mother raced around the room and began to straighten the furniture and the pictures on the walls. Now as excited as she was, Willie tried to help her, but only succeeded in knocking more things over than he was setting straight. This was not unusual, for Willie had a way of knocking things over in a room even when he was not excited.

His sister Deborah, years later, would recall: "He was always like that. He could walk into any room and immediately everything was disarranged—furniture, ashtrays, all pushed around. But we never minded the disorder. He made the place alive and exciting.

In later years, whenever he arrived, a dozen people would somehow learn about it and trail along, and soon the house would be filled."

At any rate, today his mother was much too happy to scold Willie. And that evening there was a lot of getting acquainted to be done with the tall young man who had just arrived, very trim in his uniform with the gold braid. Then, when breakfast was over the following morning, Lieutenant Halsey rose from the table and put his arm on his son's shoulder.

"Now," he said, "we're going for a little walk together. Just us menfolks."

The walk took them straight to a barber shop. When they returned home, the long yellow curls were gone. Willie's mother had a great deal to say to her husband, and sharply too, but it was too late. As far as Willie was concerned, he never missed the curls.

In the next few years he saw more of his father and a good bit of the country as well. Soon after Willie's sister Deborah was born, Lieutenant Halsey was ordered to the naval base at San Diego. This time the family followed, finding quarters in the little town of Coronado nearby. There Willie found plenty of time to wander along the beach and look out over the Pacific, dreaming of the day when he, too, would be a Navy man and go to sea like his father. But he had barely finished kindergarten when new orders sent them northward up the coast, where they lived in Vallejo, not far from San Francisco Bay. And next they moved back to Elizabeth, New Jersey, to a house on Chilton Street.

Thus Willie had a strange boyhood by ordinary standards, moving here and there, with no place really home, and with his father alternately away at sea and then at home with his family. This might have disturbed some children, but it did not seem to trouble Willie. Of course, he was always the new boy in town and at school, and it was the custom to test the newcomer's ability in battle. Once he came home from school with a bleeding scalp. His mother rushed to him, demanding to know what had happened.

"Oh," he said, "a kid hit me with a baseball bat."

"Who was it? I'm going to see his mother about that."

"Never mind," he said. "I'll take care of that guy myself."

He did. He was not a bully who picked on others, but he seemed to welcome fights. Perhaps he never actually started a fight, but, according to Colonel Woodruff, he always finished them—the winner. He had grown into a broad-chested and sturdy boy and was beginning to be called Pudge more often than Willie, though both names stayed with him. He played football and made the first team at the prep school he now attended, the Pingry School in Elizabeth.

Pudge Halsey was not a rough, tough young boy. With his father away so much of the time, his upbringing was casual. Yet it seems to have been firm when necessary, in spite of the fact his mother lavished affection on him. Sometimes she joined Lieutenant Halsey at a foreign station, and their children would be left with relatives. Somehow the family tradition of good manners came down to him, or perhaps it sprang from his own essential gentleness and warmth. Years later, his wartime chief of staff, Admiral Robert "Mick" Carney, would say of him: "He had a heart as big as a whale." These things gave him a certain self-assurance which, combined with his fighting ability and daring, made him a leader, no matter how often he had to change schools and make new friends.

A few years after the return to Elizabeth, the Navy assigned Lieutenant Halsey to teaching duty at the Academy at Annapolis, and the family moved there to join him. In those days the pay of naval officers was small, and such an assignment a coveted one, because the Navy furnished free quarters for the family. In no time at all, Pudge Halsey seems to have assembled a gang of boys about him. Years later, in early 1942, after he led a daring raid upon the Japanese-held Marshall and Gilbert islands, his name burst into headlines all over America, and many friends and boyhood playmates wrote letters to him, wanting to be remembered. One of them recalled those old days at Annapolis.

"It is from Johnny Hodges . . . who was a member of the gang of kids that used to play football on the field between the mulberry tree and Fort Severn and that often went swimming off Flock's Wharf . . . I well remember how you used to dive off the highest piles. . . ."

But Pudge Halsey's mind was not always on fighting and football and diving off the highest piles. Before the age of fifteen, he began thinking of his future. He had no doubt in his mind what he wanted to be. As far as two hundred years back there had been Halseys who captained sailing ships, one of them even being considered a pirate by some. Another had sailed an early whaler around Cape Horn. Pudge Halsey's father was a naval officer, and he intended to follow in his father's footsteps.

There remained, therefore, only the problem of getting into the Naval Academy at Annapolis. First, he needed to be nominated by a Senator or a Congressman. There were not many such nominations in the 1890's, for the Academy then graduated fewer than a hundred men a year. And how could he find a Congressman to recommend him when he had lived in half a dozen different places and had no real home?

Even if he were nominated, he still had to pass an examination. This problem did not bother Pudge Halsey as much as it did his parents, who had been looking at his grades in school. Although he was even then an avid reader, he was not a good scholar. Studying did not seem important to him when there were so many more interesting things to do.

Scholar or not, he still had a way of thinking a problem through in a straight line, so he chose the first thing first. Now a student at Swarthmore Grammar School in Philadelphia, he sat down and wrote a letter to the President of the United States. Being of a military family, he did not address him as "Dear Mr. President," but by what he considered his more important title, the rank he had held in the Civil War thirty-odd years before. Here is what he wrote at the age of fourteen.

Swarthmore Grammar School
Swarthmore, Pa.
Jan. 26, '97

Major William McKinley

Dear Sir:—

I do not suppose you remember the note some of the boys at school sent you. If you do I wish to say that my note is not of the same character. It may not be as nice to you as theirs was; although I hope sincerely it will be. I want to ask you, if you have not already promised all your appointments to the Naval Academy that you will give me one. My father is a Naval officer, and is at present navigator on the U.S.S. Montgomery. As you know as a general rule Naval officers do not have much influence, and the presidents are generally willing to give their appointments to a naval officer's son if he has not promised all of his appointments. I know people do not like to give important positions such as this is away without knowing the person they are giving them to. But then you know that a naval officer would not keep his position long if he were not the right kind of a man. I know plenty of respectable people who would testify to my good character. My father was appointed in 1869 to the Naval Academy and graduated 1873. He was appointed by Secretary Robinson [Robeson] of the Navy, who had been law partner of my grandfather. I have been with my father on shore and on ship board a great deal, and have always wanted to enter the Navy. My parents encouraged me in this desire and gave me their consent to enter if I could get the appointment. I do not know any congressman, and the appointment from the district where I live which is Elizabeth, N.J. is at present filled. I have lived three years at the Naval Academy where my father was instructor in English. I am at present a border [*sic*] of this school and am in the class that graduates in 1898. I was fourteen last October the thirtieth. My father is now senior lieutenant about 95 on the list for promotion. It is almost needless to congratulate you on your grand victory which every good American citizen sees is for the best. It has been told you so many times by men it is hardly worth while for us boys to say it.

Yours respectively,
W. F. HALSEY, JR.
Swarthmore Grammar School
Swarthmore, Pa.

He thought that would be enough, and apparently so did his father. It was now time to start working on the second problem, that matter of the examination. Lieutenant Halsey took care of that, he hoped, by entering his son in the Naval Academy Prep School run by Professor Wilmer. And the former "border" at Swarthmore settled down for a year of hard study. He could study when he had an objective.

But no word came from President McKinley. At the end of the second year the future admiral, now nearly seventeen, began to get worried. At that time one had to enter the Academy between the ages of fifteen and nineteen. How could he start his future career if he could not even get into the Navy?

So he took a desperate measure. He entered the University of Virginia as a premedical student. If he could not be a line officer in the Navy, then he would get his medical degree and join the Navy as a doctor!

At this point Anne Brewster Halsey seems to have

taken over. As Halsey recalled, his mother camped in the President's office until he promised her son an appointment. Apparently she did finally get to see McKinley, but records in the National Archives indicate that she must also have seen, or written to, every person she could think of whose recommendation might help to needle the President into action. Although the Halseys no longer lived in New Jersey, in August of 1897 letters of recommendation from the mayor of Elizabeth, the governor and the Chief Justice of New Jersey, a Congressman and several other prominent persons poured into the White House.

In 1898, a prominent Cleveland banker, later governor of Ohio and ambassador to France, wrote the President, urging an appointment for young Halsey. He mentioned as his reason that, "as you know, our bank has large real estate interests in New Jersey." More to the point, he also said that he would have mentioned the matter to Mark Hanna if he had thought it necessary, and this seems to have been a strong hint. Mark Hanna was a prominent Ohio politician who had probably done more than anyone else to get McKinley into office. In fact, opposing politicians maintained that Hanna was actually the President's boss; political cartoons of the day showed McKinley as a puppet, dancing to the strings pulled by Hanna.

This year the President at last sent a note to his Secretary of the Navy, suggesting that young William Halsey be given every possible consideration.

That did not solve the matter, however. Halsey was given an appointment as alternate. If the approved candidate failed in his physical or academic examination, or did not accept the appointment, Halsey would be next in line. But the approved candidate got the appointment.

Anne Halsey did not give up. The next year, 1899, she was still sending telegrams to the President's private secretary, whom by that time she apparently knew fairly well. In 1900 she wrote the President another letter, and so did Senator Keen. These were followed by a letter from Foster M. Voorhees, then governor of New Jersey. That same spring the sunshine broke though: Congress authorized five additional Presidential appointments to the Naval Academy, and President McKinley gave one to William F. Halsey, Jr. After considerable cramming he managed to pass the entrance examinations, and on July 7, 1900, he was sworn in.

It had taken quite a lot of doing to get Pudge Halsey started on what seems to have been his proper career, but he had finally made it. It is doubtful if any of all those who put in a word to get him there were even faintly aware of the service they had performed for their country. Except, of course, for his mother, whose pride and faith in him had made her sure of it from the beginning.

2. THE "WORST" FULLBACK

GETTING USED TO life at the Naval Academy posed no problem for Willie Halsey. He moved into barracks like the other cadets, but his .family still lived on the grounds. The discipline was greater than he had been accustomed to at boarding school, but in common with many of his classmates he found ways of getting around it from time to time. It seemed the aim of every cadet to break as many of the rules as possible. If he got caught, as he often did, then he was punished and given a certain number of demerits on his record. If he accumulated too many demerits, he could not graduate, regardless of his scholastic record. But somehow most of the cadets managed to stop just short of dismissal.

Halsey went out for football the first year, and for two years he played fullback on the scrub team. Then the regular fullback was injured, and for the following two years he played on the first team. Later in life he claimed to be "the worst fullback that ever went to the Naval Academy,"* but that is probably an exaggeration. The Academy did have rather poor teams in both those years, and in Halsey's last year they were beaten 40—5 by the Army. Pudge Halsey played the entire game. The *Philadelphia Public Ledger* of November 29, 1903 reported:

Early in the second half little Halsey electrified the Navy contingent by making the longest run of the game. Catching the ball from a kick off on his 4 yard mark he sprinted straight up the field, dodging and eluding half a dozen West Point tackles until he reached the 43 yard line, where he was brought to earth.

Even staying on the team, however, had not always been easy. There was always the matter of grades, at which Pudge Halsey seldom shone. Mechanics troubled him most. At the end of his first month of theoretical mechanics, his grade was 2.28, not even passing. In the Navy, grading differs from the usual system. A grade of 4.0 is perfect; 2.5 is just passing. His father told him in no uncertain terms that he had better give up football and spend more time on his studies. "I told him," Halsey said later, "I had rather bilge."* To bilge was Navy slang meaning to be dropped from the Academy. Furious, Lieutenant Halsey dressed down his son as only a naval officer can.

Cadet Halsey went away quietly, his mind already made up as to what he would do.

Several others in class were not doing well in theoretical mechanics, so together they asked the brighter members of the class to tutor them for the next examination.

After the examination Halsey went to his family's quarters for lunch. His father met him at the door and asked him if the marks had been posted.

"Yes sir," he answered.

"What did you make?"

"I got 3.98, sir."

His father stared at him for a full minute. "Sir," he finally asked, "have you been drinking?"*

But there were other things to learn at the Academy. Some of them Cadet Halsey found very much to his liking, and probably seamanship most of all. Much of this he learned on the cruises the cadets took each summer, which delighted him. Some cadets got seasick, but not Halsey. If he had a heart as big as a whale, he also had much of that animal's natural aptitude for water. Ships and the sea were the tools of his trade, the joy of his life, and he began very early to master both.

Today the summer cruises may take a midshipman to Europe or even farther. But at that time they were largely coastwise, as was the one in 1902, which went from Annapolis to Halifax, then back down the coast to Newport News in Virginia. Half the midshipmen went aboard the battleship *Indiana,* while the others cruised on the *Chesapeake,* a steal-hulled windjammer. The latter ship was skippered by William

F. Halsey, now a commander and head of the seamanship department at the Academy. A very abbreviated log of that cruise, as recorded in *The Lucky Bag,* or yearbook, of the Class of 1903, goes something like this:

Weighed anchor off Annapolis, 7 June 1902. Anchored that night off Cape Henry Lighthouse [or perhaps it was the following night, since this was the square-rigged sailing vessel *Chesapeake*]. On to Block Island Sound. Next anchored off the Pequot House in New London, Connecticut, and that evening the midshipmen were royally entertained by the young ladies staying at the Pequot House. On to Newport, Rhode Island, and to anchor at Narragansett Pier. There they went ashore for study at the torpedo station at Newport. When their studies were completed, they sailed across Long Island Sound to Gardiner's Bay at the tip of the island. There this contingent transferred to the old battleship *Indiana* via the latter's launch.

On this ship they held gun target practice, and steamed on to Portland, Maine, where they marched at the head of the procession in Portland's "Old Home Day" celebration. On their way from Portland to Halifax, Nova Scotia, three cadets fell overboard, one for the second time, but all were rescued. At Wellington Barracks in Nova Scotia they were dined by officers of His Britannic Majesty's forces, with many toasts being drunk to the King of England and the President of the United States.

After that the homeward voyage began. The last stop before returning to Annapolis was at Newport

News, Virginia, where the midshipmen visited the new battleships, as well as other ships of the fleet. A few days later they were back at their studies at the Academy.

The Lucky Bag of 1904, Midshipman Halsey's last year at the Academy, has a few choice words to say about life aboard the *Chesapeake,* "the good old pickle boat," whereon they battled "with all the plagues of Egypt and the rest of the earth." Many of the midshipmen were seasick on this voyage, including "Hubby"—Halsey's classmate Husband E. Kimmel, who would become the rear admiral in command at Pearl Harbor. Since Halsey was not among those afflicted, it may be presumed that he enjoyed to the fullest the month they spent later at Bar Harbor, where "hops, dinners, dances, and lawn parties . . . besieged us."

Every sailor sooner or later is faced with the problem: "Shall I get tattooed?" A few resist this urge to prove their saltiness. Halsey did not. His father had been tattooed four times, and advised against it, but the advice had little effect. On his first summer cruise, aboard the *Indiana,* he and several of his classmates decided to get tattooed with a special design which signified the Class of 1904. A coal passer, in the brig for drunkenness, engraved this design upon their shoulders. Halsey later recalled that "it was hard to tell which was filthier, he (the coal passer) or his instruments,"* and nobody knew why they did not all die of blood poisoning. Instead, all lived to regret the tattooing. At least Halsey did.

On that same cruise, aboard the *Chesapeake*, he served as royal yardman, and from that time on learned his marlinespike seamanship fast. By the time of his last, or first-class, cruise, he had worked up to port captain of the maintop, the second most responsible job in his class. He was very proud of this promotion, for he wanted to prove to his father, the captain of the ship, that he was as good an all-around sailor as the skipper. Probably he did, but he did not convince the chief master-at-arms of the Academy. When he graduated, the chief told him, with a sad shake of the head: "I wish you all the luck in the world, Mr. Halsey, but you'll never be as good a naval officer as your father!"*

The senior Halsey was unquestionably a fine officer, but he retired as a captain, five ranks below that his son later held.

Theodore Roosevelt had become President of the United States in 1901 after the assassination of McKinley. A former Assistant Secretary of the Navy, Roosevelt soon embarked upon a program of expansion for the fleet. As a result, the Class of 1904 was graduated early, in February instead of June, in order to provide enough officers for the new ships. In *The Lucky Bag* of that year, alongside the picture of a handsome, stern-faced young midshipmen, is the following:

William Frederick Halsey, Jr., Elizabeth, N.J.

"Willie," "Pudge." Lucky Bag Staff. Class Supper Committee (2). Class Crest Committee (4). Christmas Card

Committee (4). Hustlers (4). Football team (2,1). Graduation Ball Committee (2). President Athletic Association (2,1). Class German Committee (1).

"It's my opinion there's nothing 'e don't know. All the wickedness in the world is print to him."—DICKENS.

The only man in the class who can compete with General [a classmate, Arthur Gill Caffee] in the number of offices he has held. Started out in life to become a doctor and gained in the process several useful hints. Honorary member of the S.P.C.A. from having so many times saved Shubuty from persecution. A real old salt. Looks like a figurehead of Neptune. Strong sympathizer with the Y.M.C.A. movement. Everybody's friend and Brad's [his roommate, Bradford Barnette] devoted better half.

So Willie Halsey had become a naval officer at last; that is, he was a "passed midshipman." Nowadays, a Naval Academy midshipman is automatically commissioned an ensign upon graduation, but at that time the Navy required him to spend two more years at sea before becoming a full-fledged commissioned officer. Until then, he was only an "appointed" officer.

From a scholastic point of view Halsey did not exactly make it with flying colors. At the end he stood forty-third in a class of sixty-two, and that could mean slow promotion for some time to come. But it did not seem to worry Passed Midshipman Halsey. When his father took him to task for it, he shrugged his broad shoulders.

"Don't worry," he said. "Sooner or later, those

forty-two grinds ahead of me will get sick of brain fever and have to retire. Then I'll be Number One."

He was very nearly right.

Five days later Halsey went to sea on the battleship *Missouri*. He had requested this duty, and since the ship was due to leave for Guantánamo, he had to forego the month's leave usually given a midshipman upon graduation from the Academy. Thus his seagoing career began on the battleship *Missouri* and ended, forty-one years later, on quite a different battleship also named *Missouri*. The "Mighty Mo" of 1945 had nearly four times the tonnage, three times the firepower in her main battery, and almost twice the speed of Halsey's first ship.

After winter training at Guantánamo, the ship sailed back up to Pensacola, Florida, for the fleet's annual target practice. On the morning of Friday, April 13, 1904, Passed Midshipman Halsey stood on the bridge watching the practice. Suddenly he jumped at the sound of a heavy blast. A geyser of flame spouted from the top hatch of the 12-inch after gun turret. Almost at once there came a second, sharper blast. Four ninety-pound bags of powder had caught fire in the turret, and sparks had spattered down to the deck below, igniting a dozen more bags in the handling room. Thirty-one men were roasted alive.

There is nothing more dreaded aboard a ship of war than a gun-turret explosion. Coming as it did so early in his career, the effect upon Halsey was doubly lasting and profound. From that time on, he dreaded the thirteenth of every month, and lived in terror of Friday the thirteenth. As late as 1938, he wrote to an author who had sent him, for his comments, an article about the explosion:

"I would prefer not to comment for publication about that occasion. It was too harrowing an experience, it is still too vivid after thirty-four years, and it is not pleasant to bring it to mind. In addition to the many shipmates that were lost, I was a member of the Junior Officer's Mess and lost three messmates and very dear friends. As there were only eight of us in the Mess, you can imagine the effect this had on youngsters."

Halsey served aboard the *Missouri* until December 1905, but apparently the Naval Academy did not consider him "the worst fullback that ever went to the Naval Academy." Both of those years, he was detached in the autumn for temporary duty as assistant backfield coach at the Academy. The first year Navy again was beaten by Army, but the second year the two teams tied. That gave the young midshipman some consolation for the drubbings Annapolis had taken when he played on the team.

On February 2, 1906, Passed Midshipman Halsey became Ensign Halsey. It was a proud day for him when he put on that first gold stripe and became a commissioned officer in the United States Navy. He was then serving aboard a former Spanish gunboat in the Caribbean, but more exciting duty lay ahead for him, thanks to President Theodore Roosevelt.

Roosevelt said, "Walk softly and carry a big stick." His greatly enlarged Navy served as his big stick. He wanted to show it to the rest of the world and let everyone know how powerful the United States was. Accordingly, in 1907, he ordered an around-the-world cruise.

In March 1907, Ensign Halsey reported aboard the newest battleship of the fleet, the *Kansas*, which the shipbuilders were hurrying to complete in time to join the fleet on the cruise. She was commissioned and put in service the following month. For her time she was a big ship, of 16,000 tons, with a crew of 850 officers and men, and a speed of 18 knots—a ship that any Navy man would have been proud to serve upon. Like all the steamships of the time, she was a coal-burner, and put to sea with more than 2,000 tons of fuel in the hold.

That autumn the fleet sailed from Hampton Roads, Virginia, under the command of Rear Admiral Robley D. Evans, a hero of the Civil War and the Spanish-American War. It included sixteen battle-ships and five destroyers. Because Navy ships of the time were painted white, it became popularly known as the Great White Fleet.

For a young ensign nothing could have been more exciting or more rewarding than this cruise. The ships stood in at Trinidad for Christmas, went on to Rio de Janeiro and then through the Strait of Magellan and up the west coast of South America. They stopped at Valparaiso, Callao, San Diego and San Francisco, then crossed the Pacific by way of the

Hawaiian Islands to New Zealand and Australia. Everywhere they were warmly welcomed with parties and parades. At sea between these calls, it took a-while for the men to rest up from the parties ashore.

From Australia the fleet went on to Manila, (minus a few sailors who liked Australia and jumped their ships), and thence to Yokohama and Tokyo. Here they were greeted with the singing of "The Star-Spangled Banner," shouts of "Banzai!" ("May you live ten thousand years!") and the presentation of medals confirming the "good will" existing between Japan and America. Despite all this, Ensign Halsey felt that the Japanese disliked them.

One of the parties for the American officers was held aboard the battleship *Mikasa*, the flagship of Admiral Count Heihachiro Togo, who had made a torpedo attack on the Russians before the Russo-Japanese war began. Later he commanded the Japanese fleet at the Battle of Tsushima Straits, where the Russian fleet was nearly annihilated.

Among the guests were the American ambassador, Thomas J. O'Brien, and Rear Admiral Charles S. Sperry, who had relieved Admiral Evans as commander of the American fleet. At the height of the party, the Japanese officers paid their highest compliment to these two guests. Laying hands upon them, they tossed them gently into the air three times, accompanying the tosses with *banzais*.

"Naturally," Halsey wrote years later, "we had to return the compliment to Admiral Togo. We were big, and he was a shrimp, so instead of tossing him gently, we gave him three real heaves." Halsey said that if they had foreseen Pearl Harbor, "we wouldn't have caught him after the third one."*

From Japan the fleet went back to Manila, then on to Ceylon and eventually up the Red Sea and through the Suez Canal to the Mediterranean. Ensign Halsey did not get the liberty in Cairo he yearned for because a disastrous earthquake had just taken place in Messina, Sicily, and the fleet rushed there to give all possible aid.

On Washington's Birthday in 1909, the Great White Fleet steamed into Hampton Roads, and the round-the-world cruise was over. As they passed the President's yacht *Mayflower*, Roosevelt's heart was nearly bursting with pride and joy. He hoped that in every country the fleet had visited, the prestige of the United States had been increased.

From the standpoint of the Navy, the cruise had done even more. The fleet had learned to operate and fuel in distant waters. It had operated in squadrons and divisions, with every ship in formation, as would be required in modern sea warfare. The captain of each ship kept in touch with his unit commander by use of the new wireless (radio). He no longer operated alone, in supreme command, as had been true in the past. Halsey himself remembered, years later, that by the time they passed among the islands of the Philippines, the fleet had grown so efficient that he, as officer of the deck, was able for the first time to keep the *Kansas* in perfect station for the entire four hours of his watch without once speeding up or slowing down. As any naval officer short of the most experienced sea dog will agree, this is not an easy thing to do even in the best of times.

In short, this cruise marked the true beginning of the modern American Navy.

3. A YOUNG LADY FROM VIRGINIA

SHORTLY AFTER the return of the fleet to home waters, Ensign Halsey was detached from the *Kansas* and ordered to duty with the Reserve Torpedo Flotilla at Charleston, South Carolina. For him this marked the beginning of twenty-three years in torpedo boats and destroyers. He had barely reported for duty, however, before orders came sending him to Washington to be examined for promotion.

The examinations proved an ordeal. Ensign Halsey struggled through six days of questions and answers, eight hours a day, in marine and electrical engineering, international law, ordnance and gunnery, navigation and seamanship, communications, Navy regulations, and courts and boards. But in spite of his distaste for study, he once again demonstrated an ability to dig in and work when the chips were down. Of the seven ensigns who took the examinations, he was one of four who passed.

Those four also got a bonus. There happened at the time to be vacancies in the grade of lieutenant, so as soon as they were sworn in as lieutenants, junior grade, they were immediately promoted to lieutenants. The rank that would ordinarily have taken them at least two years more to reach, they received in two minutes!

The rank of lieutenant in the Navy, commonly referred to as "senior" lieutenant and equal to that of a captain in the Army, Marine Corps, and Air Force, is not exalted. Lieutenant Halsey was still a junior officer, but considering the fact that the Navy dated back his rank to February 2, 1909, just three years after he received his first commission as an ensign, it would seem that he was on his way. Apparently his performance at sea had caused someone in the Bureau of Navigation—now the Bureau of Naval Personnel—to forget about his class standing at Annapolis. The gap had begun to narrow.

Now a more exciting moment lay in store for him. Immediately upon his return to Charleston with his two stripes, he was made commanding officer of a torpedo boat, the U.S.S. *Dupont*. It was his first command.

Twenty-three years before, when the U.S. Navy commissioned its first torpedo boat, it had seemed a dangerous new weapon of war. These small craft, it was thought then, could sweep in and sink a steel-hulled battleship. To defend the big ships against enemy torpedo boats, the larger and faster torpedo-boat destroyer came into being.

But the torpedo boats did not live up to their promise. Their torpedoes could not sink a battleship, although they could damage it. They were small, frail craft, unsuited to ocean crossings or to any operations far from shore. The first of them had been only a thirty-tonner, with a speed of scarcely more than eighteen knots. The newer craft, such as the *Dupont,* were larger, but still not much by comparison with the newer destroyers, which would soon be up to a thousand tons, with a speed of more than thirty knots. These could carry more and bigger torpedoes than the torpedo boats, and they could go to sea with the fleet.

Thus the Navy discovered that the destroyers, designed as a defense against the torpedo boat, could also do the latter's job and do it better. By 1909 the destroyers were therefore swiftly replacing torpedo boats. So the twenty-six-year-old lieutenant's first command was in fact just about obsolete as a fighting ship.

This did not worry Lieutenant Halsey. Though fleet command may lie ahead for him, no true naval officer ever has a prouder moment than when he looks down from the bridge upon his first command. Furthermore, it is truly important to him, for the manner in which he handles that first command may well determine his future.

Halsey was proud of being captain of this vessel, and did not mind showing it. The first time he anchored in New York Harbor he invited his young cousin, Henry Bayard Clark, out for an afternoon's cruise. Henry, who was eighteen, did not take to the sea as his cousin did. Not long after they were out of the harbor, the vessel began to roll gently. Henry headed for the afterdeck and was very sick. His salty cousin laughed at the sight, but he was not without pity. From the galley he produced his favorite recipe, a sandwich loaded with red pepper. Henry managed to get it down—and seasickness left him.

An important matter was on the young captain's mind. Three years previously, the ship on which he was then serving had put in at the Norfolk Navy Yard for repairs. Guests came aboard, among them a young woman who was a friend of the executive officer's wife. They found Halsey, with all the authority and rigidity of a newly commissioned ensign, drilling a squad of sailors on the well deck.

"Who," asked the young lady, "is that young officer over there—the one who takes himself so seriously?"*

The exec's wife told her. Immediately something struck Ensign Halsey's cap and knocked it off. The men started to laugh, and Halsey's dignity was gone. He dismissed the squad and picked up a muff, accurately thrown by the young lady. As she reached out to recover it, Halsey pulled away from her, grinning.

"Not till you tell me your name," he said.

She obliged. She was Frances Cooke Grandy of Norfolk, a first cousin of three men who had been Halsey's close friends during his year at the University of Virginia. This seemed to him, even by the Virginia standards of the day, to make further acquaintance possible, particularly since Frances was dark-haired, pretty, and obviously had a lively sense of humor. She would be very good for a young ensign who might tend to be getting stuffy because of his gold braid.

Frances agreed, but when she introduced him to her family, the reception was cool. To them, he was just another upstart Yankee officer. One of Frances' uncles had been chief engineer of the Confederate ironclad *Merrimac*, during her battle with the Union ironclad *Monitor,* some forty years before. It seemed to Halsey that the family blamed him not only for the *Merrimac's* failure to sink the *Monitor*, but also for the defeat at Gettysburg, the burning of Richmond, and the eventual surrender at Appomattox.

Nevertheless, he did not give up. Whenever he was given leave thereafter, he spent as much time with "Fan" as her family would allow. According to Halsey, he "bombarded her with souvenirs and ardent letters from every port on the world cruise."* That, for a young man on ensign's pay, was about all he could do at the moment.

Now, however, he had had a double promotion and raise in pay. He could support a wife, at least after a fashion. So he proposed to Fan. She accepted, and the wedding was set for December 1, 1909.

Promptly, Halsey applied for a month's leave, to begin in late November. After maneuvers with the fleet off Provincetown, the *Dupont* steamed down to Jacksonville, and there the commanding officer was detached and granted his month's leave. Thanks to some of his fellow officers, on his way to the railroad station to take the train to Norfolk a brass band blaring "The Wedding March" escorted him all the way.

They were married in Christ Church in Norfolk, and their marriage lasted throughout Halsey's lifetime. Fan kept her lively sense of humor. As for her husband—no matter how high he rose, it could never be said that Bill Halsey was stuffy.

At the end of his leave Halsey was assigned to duty aboard a bigger ship, the destroyer *Lamson*, not as commanding officer but as executive officer, or second in command. After a few months of that came shore duty in Norfolk, and he and his new wife were able to take up quarters together, in a house beside the river. Here, in 1910, their daughter Margaret was born.

The shore duty lasted for over two years. Then Halsey was given command of a real fighting ship, the destroyer *Flusser*, and later additional duty commanding First Group, Torpedo Flotillas, Atlantic Fleet. Such promotions, temporary or permanent, seemed to rest easily upon the shoulders of the thirty-year-old skipper. By this time the speedy little ships were meat and drink to him; there were few if any men in the fleet who could handle a destroyer better than he.

In the summer of 1913 he was ordered to take the *Flusser to* Campobello Island, just over the border in Canada, and there pick up the Assistant Secretary of the Navy. The Secretary wanted to survey the naval installations in Frenchman Bay, off Bar Harbor and

Mount Desert Island in Maine. This was a routine enough task, except that this particular Secretary considered himself a good sailor. He asked Halsey to transit the strait between Campobello and the mainland and offered to pilot the ship.

The young captain was not happy. He knew that this man had had experience in small boats, but handling a small sailboat and a fast destroyer in narrow waters are two different things. Nevertheless, Halsey gave him the "conn," or steering control, and stood by, watching nervously.

A destroyer pivots around a point near her bridge structure. Even though her bow may be pointing directly down the channel, she may not be on a safe course. Two-thirds of her length is aft of the pivot, so her stern will swing in twice the arc of her bow. But when the Assistant Secretary made his first turn, Halsey saw him look aft and check the swing of the *Flusser's* stern. He stopped worrying then. This man knew his business; he was almost a professional sailor.

That was the beginning of a friendship between Halsey and Franklin Delano Roosevelt which lasted until the latter's death more than thirty years later.

A short time later Halsey received command of another destroyer, the *Jarvis*. This was a brand-new ship which burned oil instead of coal. To any sailor who had served aboard the dirty coal-burners, it was next to being sent straight to Paradise. To add to the young lieutenant's pleasure, the outspoken Captain William S. Sims commanded the Atlantic Destroyer Flotilla. When only a lieutenant, Sims had dared to expose the miserable record of the fleet in target practice; as a result, he had been appointed inspector of target practice by President Roosevelt. The result had been a marked improvement in the gunnery of the United States Navy. Sims ignored convention and flouted authority; he was a man after Halsey's own heart.

With such a ship and such a commander, it seemed as if there would be smooth sailing ahead for Lieutenant Halsey. For nearly a year there was.

After winter maneuvers off Guantánamo beginning in January 1914 under the watchful eye of Captain Sims, the destroyers sailed for Pensacola. There they were alerted for trouble. A revolution was under way in Mexico. Porfirio Diaz, for more than thirty years dictator of the country, had been overthrown in 1911. But his legally elected successor, Francesco I. Madero, had in turn been overthrown by General Victoriano Huerta in less than two years and later murdered by Huerta's soldiers. President Wilson refused to recognize Huerta's government, and General Venustiano Carranza rallied an army against Huerta.

In the disorder resulting from all this, on April 9, 1914, the Mexicans arrested American sailors in Tampico. Immediately, the destroyer flotilla put to sea, heading for Tampico. On the way, orders came to prepare landing forces. Unfortunately, the destroyer sailors had no khaki uniforms, which would be needed for landing. Halsey solved the problem by ordering them to boil their whites in coffee. As a result, he said, the *Jarvis* "smelled like a Greasy Spoon."*

They did not need the uniforms after all since it was decided by the time they arrived off Tampico to provoke no further "incidents" by landing. The destroyers lay offshore while American refugees came out in smaller vessels and boarded the destroyer tender *Dixie*. Marines and sailors landed at Veracruz on April 21, and eventually the destroyers were ordered there.

The ships took turns in making a mail run to Galveston, Texas. One day before the turn of the *Jarvis,* a fireman named Frank Harrison reported aboard for duty. Two hours later he jumped ship and came back roaring drunk. When the master-at-arms tried to put him under arrest, he jumped over the side into shark-infested waters. Halsey had searchlights turned on and sent out small boats to comb the harbor waters, but there was no sign of the missing sailor. Finally, they discovered that Harrison had climbed back aboard and hidden under the after torpedo tubes.

They hauled him out and locked him up for the night. The next morning he was brought before captain's mast. Halsey gave him a summary court-martial, making him a prisoner at large until such time as the court-martial could be convened.

By this time the *Jarvis* was on its way to Galveston. During that day and the following night, Harrison gave no further trouble. But when they had picked up the mail and were under way for Veracruz, the master-at-arms came to Halsey to report that the fireman had jumped ship again at Galveston—and again had come back aboard drunk and obstreperous.

This time he was accompanied by a fellow sailor named Conly. (Neither of these names is the true one, since both men may still be living.)

The captain had Harrison brought before him. "If you want to be treated like a man," Halsey said, "act like a man. If you want to be treated like a mad dog, act like one, and by Heaven, I'll chain you up!"

"Aye, aye, sir," Harrison answered meekly. "I'll behave myself."*

But within a short time both men were up on deck again, with Harrison still wildly drunk and a danger both to himself and his shipmates. True to his word, Halsey had the two chained in a storeroom, with both hand and leg irons. Somehow the pair got hold of a file that mysteriously lay nearby, and sawed themselves free. There was strong suspicion that a shipmate, enjoying the excitement, gave them a hand. Later a petty officer, commenting upon the fact that Harrison seemed to stay drunk for hours after he had been back on board, suggested that someone might have passed him liquor through one of the air ports or ventilators overhead.

At any rate, this time Halsey had them spread-eagled for the night, with their hands chained to one stanchion and their feet to another. This time they did not break free. Not until the following morning did Halsey learn that the only two stanchions where spread-eagling was possible had a low hatch-coaming between them. Hence the two must have spent a painful night.

When the ship reached Veracruz the captain had the two men transferred to a battleship's brig and requested a trial by general court-martial. A general court-martial can award stiffer punishments than can a summary, even including the death penalty. At that time such a court-martial could be convened only by the Secretary of the Navy.

Generally speaking, Halsey's record shows that he was lenient with his men. The log of the U.S.S. *Benham,* a destroyer he commanded in World War I. is a fair example. At a time when punishments of enlisted men were common, he punished few, and most of them mildly. In sharp contrast was Frank Jack Fletcher, who relieved him in May 1918. Half an hour after the latter took command, he held captain's mast and awarded one general court-martial, one bad-conduct discharge, and seven summary courts-martial—some of these for offenses committed while Halsey was commanding officer. Halsey nevertheless expected top performance from every man at sea, though if any one in his command got into trouble ashore he would back him to the limit. This earned his a vast loyalty among the men who served under him.

The fact was that Harrison had been in trouble, or at least of no use to the Navy, in every station he had served on. On the *Jarvis* he had stolen stamps and tobacco from a shipmate's locker under the eyes of three witnesses. Before his confinement, the ship's doctor examined him, doubting his sanity.

He was charged at the court-martial with theft, conduct to the prejudice of good order and discipline, drunkenness incapacitating him for the proper performance of duty, and willful destruction of public property. He was convicted and sentenced to five years in Portsmouth Naval Prison, to be followed by a dishonorable discharge from the Navy.

Halsey assumed the matter was closed. But he was wrong. He did not know that Frank Harrison was writing letters from the prison to his stepfather, telling a tale of inhuman treatment for fancied misdeeds that did not fit the facts. The stepfather believed the tale. At once he wrote to the Secretary of the Navy, and in time the letter reached the desk of Secretary Josephus Daniels.

The letter spoke of "trumped-up" charges and stated that the stepfather expected "you to right the wrong, by punishing the officers in charge for giving a boy of his age and 'statue' such treatment." He "vouched for the boy's [Harrison was twenty-six] good behavior as a civilian," and suggested that if the Navy was not satisfied with him, they could just forget the whole thing and send him back home!

Through a friend he was also able to get word of the matter to Newton D. Baker, mayor of Cleveland, a prominent politician and soon to become Secretary of War. Baker promised to write the Secretary of the Navy, and did so, although his letter was not at all critical. It concluded with the phrase, "I need not say that I do not request unjust mercy any more than I fear unmerciful justice from you."

These letters—the stepfather wrote more than one—caused Daniels to decide to review the case personally. A few days later, Lieutenant Halsey received a curt letter from Daniels, actually an order, stating: "You will make a full report of all the circumstances in connection with the alleged misconduct of Frank Harrison, fireman second class."

As if that were not enough to make any young naval officer feel disaster approaching, included with the letter was a personal note to Halsey from a friend in the department. The note warned him to be very careful with his answer, since the Secretary of the Navy had hinted that he intended to make an example of Lieutenant Halsey!

The name of the "friend" is not mentioned in his own recollections, nor does it appear in the records of the case in the National Archives. It is reasonable to speculate, however, that it could have been Franklin Delano Roosevelt, Assistant Secretary of the Navy. Whoever it was, he was a true friend indeed.

Halsey sweated over the reply, writing one draft after another, showing it to friends and asking for their comments. He felt that he had been right, but how could he convince the man who was out to make an example of him?

In the final draft, he pointed out that he had fully explained the measures taken against Harrison in the charges that the Secretary had already seen before himself ordering the court-martial. He also noted various inaccuracies in the stepfather's letter. He then repeated what Harrison and Conly had done, and the measures he had taken. In conclusion he said:

"The absolute disregard of orders by these men caused all temperate measures taken for their confinement to fail, and I was forced to resort to irons to insure their safe custody, the safety of the ship, and the proper maintenance of discipline aboard the vessel I commanded."

Halsey mailed the letter and, figuratively speaking, held his breath. It was a good thing he did not actually hold it until the Secretary answered, because the Secretary never did. But Daniels did review the case. Perhaps because of pressure brought to bear by Harrison's stepfather through one of his Senators, the Secretary reduced the five-year sentence to two years. In fact, Harrison was released after only sixteen months, which included the time he had spent in confinement while awaiting trial and approval of the sentence.

Nevertheless, Halsey's naval career no longer was in danger.

4. OUTWITTED BY EXPERTS

AFTER THE Mexican troubles quieted down, the destroyers went north to Norfolk where Halsey rejoined his wife and daughter Margaret.

His life ashore was interrupted in August, however, when World War I began in Europe. The United States remained neutral, but harbors and the coast-line had to be patrolled. The *Jarvis* was assigned to patrol outside New York Harbor. It seemed to be routine duty, but it had problems that demanded fast thinking and good seamanship.

For example, one job was to keep watch on a yacht, the *Winchester*, which was so fast that the government expected Germany to buy her and try to take her abroad. This would have been a violation of American neutrality. To complicate matters, a British warship took up patrol outside the three-mile limit with the idea of stopping the *Winchester* if she put out of the harbor into international waters. Then a dense fog shut down.

There was no radar in those days, of course. The only certain way a ship could get a fair idea of its position at sea was by getting a celestial fix with a sextant. Another, less sure, way was by dead reckoning—that is, by estimating from the ship's course and speed and the drift of current how far it had gone and in what direction since the last time a celestial fix had been made.

On the morning of the dense fog, the *Jarvis* had been taking part in maneuvers with other destroyers over a 600-mile run on various courses at various speeds. Dead reckoning cannot be accurate under such circumstances. The ship was supposed to finish her run off Sandy Hook Lightship, outside the New York Harbor entrance. But because of the weather, Halsey had been unable to get a single celestial fix during the entire run.

At that point the *Jarvis,* with nobody aboard knowing quite where she was, popped out of the thick weather and into something approaching broad daylight. There, dead ahead, stood a strange warship! It was the British patrol.

In wartime, the best gunner is apt to be trigger-happy in such a situation. Both ships expected the other to open fire before there was time for proper identification. Halsey acted instantly, ordering right full rudder to swing the *Jarvis* back into the heavy weather.

That forestalled the danger of a mistaken battle,

but it brought him into fresh danger. It was something he did not see, and he did not know what it was. He simply had a hunch of impending disaster.

Halsey did not stop to analyze. He called to the engine room: "Full speed astern!" When the ship had stopped its forward movement, Halsey spotted a fishing boat through the murk.

"What's our position?" he called out.

"If you keep going for half a mile," the fisherman yelled back, "you'll be right in the middle of the Fire Island Life Saving Station!"*

What had saved the *Jarvis* from disaster may have been only a good sailor's hunch. More likely, Halsey felt later, it was a feeling of drag from the shoaling water, or the sudden appearance of large swells off the stern.* At any rate he had acted—and acted fast— twice in the space of a few minutes.

A naval captain who runs his ship aground can get a black mark on his record which may never be erased. Admiral Arleigh (31-Knot) Burke, himself a fine destroyer sailor, once said that the difference between a good officer and a poor one is ten seconds. If so, Halsey passed the test twice in that one day.

In July of the following year, Halsey being due for a change to shore duty, was offered a choice. Because of the war in Europe, the Navy wanted its forces at full strength and was establishing recruiting stations in various northeastern cities. Halsey could have recruiting duty or go to the Naval Academy. Probably bearing in mind the free quarters at

Annapolis—no small item when trying to raise a family on lieutenant's pay—Halsey chose the Naval Academy. Another consideration was the fact that Fan was execting another child in September.

The Academy assigned him to the discipline department. He thought that, after eleven years of handling enlisted men, he would have no trouble with midshipmen. The night the midshipmen returned to the Academy, Halsey had a hunch that the first man he would have to put on report would be the son of a friend. His inspection after supper took him into a room filled with smoke, and smoking was contrary to regulations. Halsey asked who was in charge.

"I am, sir," a midshipman answered.

"Your name?"

"Midshipman Macklin, sir."

"Are you a son of General Macklin?"

"Yes, sir."

"I knew it!" Halsey cried.*

He had forgotten that to midshipmen this matter of discipline was a game to be played between them and the duty officer. If they could break a rule and not get caught, they had scored a point. Those who managed successfully and often to break the regulations were considered "touge." This might consist of wearing nonregulation trousers with side pockets, of Frenching into town—that is, going in without permission—or of a variety of other offenses, depending upon the ingenuity of the cadet. In Halsey's time, where he was a plebe or fourth-classman, one of the most touge cadets of all was a first-classman who Frenched regularly after supper and was never caught. He also stood at the top of his class scholastically. His name was Ernest J. King, and during World War II he became Chief of Naval Operations—top man in the Navy—and a fleet admiral.

One of the first things that Halsey did after his early experience was to try to have the regulation against smoking changed. He knew from his own experience as a cadet that this rule could not be enforced, and so he considered it a poor regulation. The medical officers objected, but eventually the rule was changed—though not while Halsey was in the discipline department of the Academy.

He still had to cope with a genius in the Class of 1916 who managed to rig up some sort of smoke consumer in his shower. The smoke just vanished; Halsey was never able to figure out how. There was also another genius in a later class who was able to establish some sort of mysterious control over all the bells, buzzers, lights, and even the elevators in Bancroft Hall, the midshipmen's dormitory. He operated all these electrical devices at his own whim, so that bells rang mysteriously, lights went off and on, and empty elevators went up and down.

Admiral Robert "Mick" Carney was a member of the Class of 1916. He denies being the unknown genius, and also remembers a somewhat different Lieutenant Halsey than the stern disciplinarian one might have expected. Carney says of Halsey:

"When he was on duty at the Naval Academy he tempered necessary disciplinary severity with humor and tolerance. On his inspection rounds, in the midshipmen's quarters, his dangling and clanking sword could be heard in ample time to get things in order before he arrived—which achieved the desired result without resort to punishment."

If Halsey's superiors knew about his departure from the tradition of the harsh, tough naval officer, they seem not to have held it against him. When Congress passed a bill in 1916 to enlarge the Navy, he became eligible for promotion to the rank of lieutenant commander. After another long boning session, night and day, he passed the examination and was promoted. The pay raise proved helpful to a young officer who had had a son added to his family the preceding September in the person of William Frederick Halsey III.

By this time Halsey had a fresh worry. It soon became evident that America would be getting into the war in Europe. He had had enough of watching over midshipmen, and when war came he wanted to be at sea. Nevertheless, when war came the following April, he was still at Annapolis. Instead of being sent to sea, he was made director of athletics and also given the job of drilling a class of Naval Reserve officers—young men just out of college.

September and October of 1917 came and went, and he was still ashore. Finally, in November, a friend tipped him off that Admiral Sims, now in command of American naval forces in Europe, had sent the Navy Department a list of officers he wanted in his command. Sims had not forgotten the young destroyer skipper of a few years back; Halsey's name was on the list. He went at once to see the commandant of the Academy. At last, after a relief was found for him, he was detached in December from the Naval Academy with orders to proceed to Queenstown, Ireland, for duty with destroyers.

Now he would be fighting the war.

5. SUBMARINE WARFARE

WORLD WAR I was not a naval war in the sense of ships fighting in great battles, as they had done in past wars and would again in World War II. Even before the United States entered the war on the side of the Allies, the fleet of Great Britain alone was more powerful than that of Germany and her allies together. The Germans, quite aware of this, only once sent their High Seas Fleet out to do battle with the British Grand Fleet.

That was in May 1916, at the Battle of Jutland. Though the British lost more in tonnage of ships in that battle than did the Germans, the German fleet retired to the security of its base at Helgoland, and the battleships—dreadnoughts, they were then called— did not come out again. Some of the fast cruisers managed to slip past the British blockade and go out to raid the shipping lanes; some were already at sea, in the Pacific and Atlantic, when the war began, and these caused plenty of trouble for the Allied Powers.

The Germans at this point fell back on their submarine fleet, as they had been planning to do all along. Up to this time the submarine had not been greatly used in naval warfare, but the Germans had built up a sizable fleet of these undersea craft. They could not defeat the British Navy, but that was not necessarily important. The Allied Powers, especially Britain, depended upon shipping to bring them food and ammunition and all the other supplies a warring nation needs. Most of these things had to come from the United States. Accordingly, the submarines set about trying to sink the ships bringing supplies to Great Britain.

Toward the end of 1916 submarines were sinking around 300,000 tons of shipping per month. In April 1917, they reached a record of 875,000 tons. It was beginning to hurt; if it had kept on, Britain would have been throttled. But by this time the British Royal Navy was beginning to work out means to fight the submarine menace with destroyers and smaller subchasers which escorted the convoys through the danger zones. They did not have all the underwater sound devices to detect submarines which were used in World War II, except for hydrophones to locate them by the sound of the engines. They did have depth charges to let loose on submarines, and they sank several of them. Sometimes hydroplanes were used to spot submarine targets for destroyers.

What Britain needed was not more battleships, but more destroyers. Fortunately, America had them—

and was building more. One of the Navy's first acts after the declaration of war on Germany in April 1917 was to flash a message to the Boston Navy Yard ordering six destroyers under way for Britain. In a short time the destroyers were knifing their way across the North Atlantic bound for Queenstown, Ireland. They arrived there on May 4, 1917. The British commander to whom they reported expected that these little ships would need repairs and that their crews would need rest after the rough crossing. He asked the American commander when he would be, as the British put it, "in all respects ready for sea and to engage the enemy."

"We are ready now, sir," Commander Joseph K. Taussig answered. "That is, as soon as we finish refueling."

They arrived none too soon. The submarine menace had resulted in strict rationing of food in Britain.

By the time Lieutenant Commander Halsey arrived in Queenstown in January 1918, the situation had improved somewhat. The destroyers were beginning to exact a heavy toll in German submarines. There still remained plenty to be done, however, and Halsey was put to work immediately. He was first assigned to temporary duty aboard the destroyer *Duncan* under another commanding officer to learn the job of hunting submarines. For the next fex weeks they escorted convoys out of French, English and Irish ports, taking them 500 miles to the westward where they would be reasonably safe from German submarines. There the destroyers would pick up an east-bound convoy from the States and escort it into port. Normally they spent five days at sea, then three days in Queenstown. They took five days off to clean boilers after every fifth trip.

Early in February Halsey was promoted to the temporary rank of commander, and within two weeks had his own destroyer, the *Benham*. She was a fine ship, with an excellent crew, Halsey's proudest command to date. He expected now to sink German submarines by the score.

There were plenty of German submarines around, but the problem was to find them. Weeks followed in which the *Benham* escorted convoys in all weather, rescued seamen from sinking ships, spotted a floating spar that was probably a German decoy with a mine attached, and once dropped a depth charge with no visible results.

Although not the most exciting way to fight a war, neither was it exactly dull. Running through the crowded convoy lanes without lights on a black night or a fogbound day required alertness every moment and the sharpest kind of seamanship. These things the skipper of the *Benham* had, and so did his crew. He had a sharp-eyed quartermaster, a full-blooded Indian, who one morning stopped Halsey just in time from giving the order to open fire on a submarine dead ahead of them. She had failed to answer his challenging signal, but the quartermaster, looking through the telescope, identified her correctly as an American submarine.

The destroyers of that time were less than half the size and tonnage of modern ones, and the rough seas of the North Atlantic could all but bury them. It took a tough man indeed to serve on "tin cans," yet few who had once served aboard them would think of asking for easier duty. A destroyer man walked with a special swagger; from danger, rough weather and crowded quarters shared, there grew a comradeship between officers and men. Spit and polish was the rule in those days, but not aboard a destroyer, where the uniform of the day was likely to be what most suited the weather. Even thirty-five-year-old Commander Halsey, raised in Annapolis traditions, would proudly be photgraphed aboard his ship wearing his old Annapolis sweater with the big "N" on it, the sweater buttoned wrong and beneath it a nondescript shirt open at the neck.

Perhaps this service made Halsey the kind of man he later proved to be. If not, it certainly brought out those qualities which were already latent in him. He never became a "go-by-the-book" officer. In a later war, he would be the admiral who ordered his officers to take off their neckties, partly because they wasted too much valuable time in the morning in tying them. He hated red tape, even the red tape of his own beloved Navy. He demanded top performance from the men who served under him, but he had no love for rules and regulations if they got in the way of fast performance. More than once he broke the rules, sometimes to the annoyance of his superiors.

Certainly he was getting plenty of experience, if he needed it, in handling a ship in all kinds of weather. One day in June of 1918 he found himself SOPA— Senior Officer Present Afloat—in command of two

American destroyers and two British sloops. He had a fine time ordering them around, and said later that he "was as proud as a dog with two tails."*

But as far as gaining a reputation as a killer of German submarines, Commander Halsey had no luck at all. On July 8, after he had left the *Benham* to take command of the destroyer *Shaw,* he thought he had something. The *Shaw* dropped depth charges which brought up oil—often an indication that a submarine has been hit.

According to that day's log of the *Shaw,* the depth charges also brought up a "water breaker [cask] which was found to be anchored to a length of manila spliced into a wire. Breaker had the following painted on it in white letters: 'S.S. *Reserve,* c/o N.S.O. Aberdeen.' " They lowered a whaleboat to investigate, and found that the whole thing seemed to be made fast to something on the bottom.

Halsey notified Headquarters, and two British trawlers with hydrophones came out to listen for sounds of a submarine below. Oil continued to come to the surface in some quantity, but the moored water cask had mysteriously disappeared! The trawlers could find no indication of a submarine.

Halsey's guess was that the *Shaw* had hit a submarine at periscope depth before she could dive, and that the depth charge had torn the buoy loose from her outer hull structure. He thought that somehow the submarine had been able to drag it back down and through some sort of watertight opening. But it was only a guess, and a rather wild one. The truth would never be known.

All he really did know was that he came in for considerable ribbing from his fellow officers. They called him "the Duke of Aberdeen" and "the Count of Coningberg," and even made up a song that ran:

> Last night over by Aberdeen,
> I saw a German submarine.
> The funniest sight I ever seen
> Was old Bill Halsey's submarine.*

A few weeks later Halsey was detached from his ship and returned to the States for leave and command of a new destroyer. Before she had been put into commission, the war ended. The tale of the vanishing buoy, however, should not serve as the last word on Halsey's first war. Even though he sank no submarines, he and his fellow destroyer men learned a great deal about how to fight a war, and the destroyers in World War II put that knowledge to good use. This included such matters as how to hunt for submarines on the basis of Intelligence reports and, perhaps even more important, the handling of repairs on a round-the-clock basis so that the destroyers were always ready to put to sea on call.

The Navy awarded Halsey a Navy Cross "for distinguished service in the line of his profession as Commanding Officer of the U.S.S. *Benham* and the U.S.S. *Shaw*, engaged in the important, exacting, and hazardous duty of patrolling the waters infested with enemy submarines and mines, in escorting and protecting vitally important convoys of troops and supplies through these waters, and in offensive and defensive action, vigorously and unremittingly prosecuted against all forms of enemy naval activity."

Halsey maintained that the Navy Cross was handed out rather freely to commanding officers during that war, so that it did not mean as much as when it was awarded in World War II.

His new ship, the *Yarnall*, was a 1,200-tonner, and the latest thing in destroyers. At his own request, he made his shakedown cruise as an escort to the ship on which President Wilson sailed to France to help work out the terms of the peace treaty with Germany and her allies. The *Yarnall* was kept in Europe for six months, mostly on messenger duty. In January of 1919 it made a run to Portugal.

The night it left Lisbon was black; there was a long, rolling swell in the estuary at the lower reaches of the Tagus River, which forms the harbor of Lisbon. As Elmer Dunbar, one of the sailors aboard the *Yarnall*, remembered it:

"There was a terrible storm. Halsey was given orders to go out in spite of it. He didn't want to, but he loosened the ropes and started."

It was necessary to keep one of the bow anchors ready for letting go in case of trouble, so a working party composed of an officer and three sailors stayed in the bow. As soon as the ship cleared the harbor mouth, Halsey ordered the anchor secured, and the working party started aft. Just as the men reached the forecastle, the *Yarnall* dipped her nose into a heavy sea.

"Three men [of the working party] were washed

overboard and lost," Dunbar recalls. "Halsey swore after that he'd use his own judgment on weather conditions when the lives of his men were at stake. There's a real man."

There was never again an accidental death on a ship under his immediate command.

6. BEATING THE BATTLESHIPS

AFTER WORLD WAR I the United States Navy fell upon hard times. Congress saw no need to maintain a big navy, and Congress probably reflected the mood of the majority of the American people.

Not long after the war the United States had the largest destroyer force in the world—316 ships in all. Of these a few were converted into minelayers, and all but about 100 of the remainder went into mothballs. Operating funds for seaworthy ships were cut to the bone; in order to go to sea at all ships had to maintain a speed that would use the least fuel. One destroyer officer said, "This steaming develops eight-knot minds in thirty-knot ships." The number of bluejackets also had to be drastically reduced. In time, economy plus naval disarmament treaties resulted in the Navy being forced for a while to retire automatically the lower half of each graduating class at Annapolis. It would have been a poor time for a future Halsey to be graduating.

Nevertheless, the Navy kept functioning. Destroyers had earned an important place in the fleet. In the summer of 1919 the *Yarnall* was ordered to join the new Pacific Fleet being formed. Halsey, still a destroyer man and still in command, went with her, but now he had additional duty as division commander. A destroyer division, which now is normally composed of two to four ships, then included six.

In spite of shortages of manpower and money, and thanks to good commanders, destroyers practiced their maneuvers until their men considered them the hottest ships in the fleet. One of the ship captains who contributed his bit to this was Commander Halsey, who worked out a fast anchoring device. It was simple enough—a matter of slowing to two-thirds speed when approaching the anchorage, then backing at full speed as soon as the anchor was dropped. It was a smart-looking maneuver, and also sensible, the best way to get light ships placed at their anchorages. At slower speeds they did not handle properly. When he explained this method to other division commanders, they laughed at him, saying it would never work. But he trained his own division in the practice, and soon the others had to follow suit or look like sloppy sailors by comparison.

In January of 1920 the Navy ordered the *Yarnall* to the China station. Since Halsey had now been at sea for two years and was due for shore duty soon, he was transferred to command of another destroyer, the *Chauncey,* based on the Pacific Coast. Up to then, in eleven years of commanding ships, Halsey had never suffered a bad collision. That fact no doubt helped to account for his rather regular promotions and his standing with the top brass.

But his luck ran out on a squadron cruise to Pearl Harbor. A weakness in the *Chauncey*'s boilers caused pressure to fall so low that the ship had to be stopped at once. Halsey ordered the breakdown flag hoisted, but the wind fouled it in the rigging. He ordered emergency blasts on the whistle, but there was no steam.

The destroyer *Aaron Ward* was bearing down, and its watch officer, a green ensign, failed to recognize the danger. He slowed his ship but kept on coming. Halsey, without power or steering control, could only stand on the bridge and wait for the worst.

The bow of the *Aaron Ward* sliced through the thin plates of the *Chauncey* and drove eight feet into her steering-engine room, flooding it. Halsey rushed below to inspect the damage. The starboard engine was disabled and the starboard cables to the tiller had been severed.

"Anybody hurt?" Halsey asked.

"Nobody, sir," the engineering watch officer answered. "All present and accounted for."

Halsey heaved a sigh of relief. "That's all that matters," he said. "We can sweat this can into Pearl somehow."

He meant it, too. As long as there were no casualties, he would not worry about his own record. Nor, apparently, did his superiors. He soon took command of another ship, the *John F. Burnes*. When she proved to use too much fuel for the economy-minded

Navy and was put into reserve, he became commanding officer of the *Wickes*. He remained a division
commander throughout, and the following spring
would receive a temporary promotion to squadron
commander. This was due to bring more frowns from
the admirals than the collision of the *Ward* and
Chauncey.

In the early spring of 1921 orders came for the
squadron to simulate a torpedo attack on four battleships. Just before the exercise illness overtook the
squadron commander, and Halsey was given temporary command. The squadron included three divisions
of six destroyers each, plus the flagship, the biggest
command he ever had held.

His only instructions were to proceed to a
position about 30,000 yards from the battleships
and stand by for a signal to begin his attack. This,
for a man of Halsey's determination and daring,
offered a lot of leeway. He intended to take advantage of it. He put two divisions of destroyers in
parallel columns only 1,000 yards apart and ordered
the third division to trail them, ready to take an intercepting course if the "enemy" battleships tried to
avoid the others.

When the signal to attack came, Halsey headed
his own destroyer straight for the battleship column.
As the distance began to close, he ordered the entire
squadron to make smoke. Thus all but the leading
destroyers would be hidden.

The Commander of Destroyers, Pacific Fleet,

Captain Pratt, was on the bridge of the *Wickes* as an observer. He turned to Halsey.

"What do you intend to do?" he asked.

"What's the limit?" Halsey asked.

"The sky."

"If the battleships maintain their course and speed," Halsey said, "I intend to put them between my two columns and fire at them from both sides."*

This kind of maneuvering took alert crews and fine ship-handlers on every destroyer. When they closed, the destroyer columns would each be only 500 yards from the battleships, which is not considered much leeway when fast ships are headed toward each other at sea. Halsey headed his own ship on its collision course with the battleship column until he reached the firing point, only 3,000 yards from the leading ship. Then he ducked back into his own smoke. His flagship carried no torpedoes, because there were not enough to go around.

But he had at least marked the firing point. As each destroyer reached that same point, she fired twice—a total of thirty-six torpedoes, each with a practice head. Of the thirty-six, there were twenty-two hits.

The way such exercises had previously been carried out, firing from a considerable distance, no damage would have been done. The torpedoes' practice heads were of soft metal noses to lessen the impact, and the torpedoes were expected to be usable again.

But as Halsey did it, things turned out differently.

Intent on making a daring close-in attack it order to show what a courageous destroyer man could do against battleships in actual war, Halsey had not considered one thing. At that time torpedo engines were driven by compressed air. On a long run most of the air would be gone by the time a torpedo arrived, but since the range was constantly closing, the last of these were fired from 700 yards. When they struck, they were still loaded with compressed air. As a result, they exploded.

The explosions were not as great, of course, as if the torpedoes' noses had been loaded with TNT, but they were great enough to cause considerable damage. The flagship of the vice admiral commanding took a hit that ruptured her plating and flooded her paint locker. Another ship had two torpedoes explode among her propellers and put her out of commission. A torpedo smashed into the steering-engine room of a third ship, blew all her circuit breakers and paralyzed most of her electrical gear. Only one of the four battleships escaped damage.

In a minute and a half, Halsey's destroyers had done a million and a half dollars' worth of damage!

The battleship men were understandably furious. They were even more so when they got back to their base and saw this headline in the newspaper:

DESTROYERS DECISIVELY DEFEAT BATTLESHIPS

Another exercise of the same kind had been scheduled for the following day. Before the destroyers got under way, however, Halsey and Captain Pratt received orders to report aboard the flagship of the admiral. No record is available of what was said, but it was obviously a good deal and spoken in strong language. Halsey may have been in danger of court-martial. In any event, he defended himself in very few words:

"I was ordered to attack. I attacked."

Apparently that saved him from serious trouble. He was told, nevertheless, not to repeat the performance of the previous day. No more battleships were damaged.

Once again, perhaps because of his bold methods, Halsey's standing in the Navy did not seem to have been damaged. Soon thereafter the *Wickes* received the Navy's award for general excellence, and another ship in his division won the top trophy for destroyer gunnery. The commander of such a division could scarcely receive a black mark on his record. At any rate, at that time he made permanent commander and was ordered to shore duty in Naval Intelligence in Washington. He would not be back with destroyers again for nearly three years.

7. HALSEY TAKES TO THE AIR

IT WAS the rule in the Navy in those days that a career officer should be broadly trained, suited to perform any duty that the service demanded. In the next few years Commander Halsey would be getting plenty of such training. He served for a year on his first duty in Washington and hoped it would be his last. Disliking paperwork, he soon grew impatient to be off again. When he heard that a relief was needed for the naval attaché in Germany, he quickly volunteered. In the autumn of 1922 he sailed for Europe with his wife and family.

Halsey did a good job in this assignment. After a while he was given additional duty as naval attaché to the embassies in Norway, Denmark and Sweden. He also succeeded in arranging for the purchase of a German invention, a stereoscopic range finder which the Navy found much better than the one it had been using.

All his years at sea had not made of Halsey the rough sea dog so often pictured, though in salty talk and rough language he could compete with anyone. When he felt that someone in his command had been doing a job badly, he could blister a man in a way the man never would forget. Under other circumstances, however, Halsey showed courtesy and kindliness. Perhaps it was because he usually liked people and could laugh at his own weaknesses. Admiral Carney said of him: "Halsey could get along with anyone." While this may be a slight exaggeration from a man who admired him deeply, almost anyone who served with him would say much the same.

In July 1924 Halsey went back to sea in command first of the *Dale* and next the *Osborne*, two destroyers then in European waters. Late in 1925 he and his family returned home and he served for a year as executive officer of the battleship *Wyoming*. This service may have been the Navy's way of grooming him for the rank of captain; he was selected for that rank a few months later and took his examination. In February 1927 his promotion came through.

Meanwhile he had been ordered back to the Naval Academy as commanding officer of the *Reina Mercedes*, an old Spanish cruiser which was a prize from the Spanish-American War. This old hulk served as a receiving ship for the Academy and also as a prison ship for cadets caught Frenching. The command did not seem of great importance, yet it marked a turning point in Halsey's naval career.

In the spring of 1927, the *Reina Mercedes* became the base of the Academy's first permanent aviation detail. Halsey did not like being in charge of something he did not understand, so he asked the officer in charge of the aviation detail, Lieutenant Dewitt C. Ramsey, to educate him. "Fine!" Ramsey said. "Let's go flying!"*

From that day on, Halsey flew as often as Ramsey or his executive officer would give him a ride. In time they let him handle the controls. As he said, he was soon "eating, drinking, and breathing aviation."* Eventually his interest came to the attention of the Chief of the Bureau of Navigation, who offered him the opportunity to enter the Navy flight school at Pensacola. Halsey jumped at the chance.

There was sound reason behind this offer. Even in 1930 naval aviation had not gone far beyond its adolescent stage. The first aircraft carrier, the *Langley*, was not commissioned until 1922 and was only a converted fueling ship. Although the Naval Aeronautic Station at Pensacola was established in 1914, Annapolis graduates did not show much interest in aviation. Those who studied it tended to be cadets with the lowest grades. The picture changed after 1916, however, and by the late 1920's plenty of bright young naval officers were winning their pilot's wings. What the Navy now lacked were trained senior officers who could command these young men and the carriers being built.

There a man like Halsey, interested in aviation, fit in. Unfortunately, this time he could not qualify. He took the physical examination, but failed the eyesight test. He waited a week and tried again, and again he failed. He had to give up—and supposed it was for good.

In June 1932 he was ordered to the command of Destroyer Squadron 14 in the Atlantic Fleet. Though glad to be back at sea again in his favorite ships, he had by no means lost interest in flying. Planes had now become an integral part of the fleet and spotted torpedo practice runs for the destroyers. Part of the time Halsey watched from his bridge; the rest of the time he flew with the pilots and watched from the air.

Two years later he went as a student to the Naval War College at Newport, then spent a year at the Army War College in Washington in preparation for high command. Halsey had said good-by to destroyers for the last time.

Toward the end of his year at the Army War College, in 1934, his second chance came in aviation. The Chief of the Bureau of Aeronautics, Rear Admiral Ernest King, offered him command of the carrier *Saratoga* if he would first take the aviation observer's course at Pensacola—which would not require his passing the difficult eye test.

Halsey was ready to agree at once, but he felt that he had to consult his wife. Fan did not feel happy about it, but eventually she gave her consent. She was a wise woman; no doubt she knew she could not keep Bill Halsey out of the air.

Fifty-one years old, a grandfather, and a captain in the Navy, Halsey settled his family for the summer and drove south to Pensacola to begin a new career.

Captain Halsey attacked his new assignment with his customary enthusiasm, mixed with a reasonable amount of common sense. After a few days of flying around with his instructor, he decided he wanted to be changed from a "student observer" to a "student pilot." Someone must have "neglected" to give him that eye test, because he became a student pilot. But if he earned a passing mark there, he did not get it with Fan. When he finally got up enough nerve to write his wife and tell her of the change, she was furious—and no doubt worried as well.

"What do you think the old fool is doing now!" she exclaimed to their daughter. "He's learning to fly! It must be that flying is the only thing left that will made him feel young again. He can't turn somersaults on the ground any more, so he's going to turn them up in the air. Did you ever hear such a thing? It's all your fault! You made him a grandfather!"*

Halsey felt that if he were going to command a carrier, he ought to know what a pilot's problems were and what went on in his mind. This kind of thinking later made the flyers who served under him in the Pacific swear by Halsey. They knew that the man on top was not just another seagoing admiral, but a man who understood them and had their best interests at heart.

At any rate, he learned to fly. He was the last one in his class to solo, and one of Pensacola's customs was to dunk the last soloist in each class. When he taxied his seaplane back to the ramp, his classmates were waiting for him. But most were ensigns, and the captain's eagles on his collar made them hesitate.

Halsey looked at them and grinned. They hesitated no longer; he went into the harbor just like any young ensign.

It cannot be said that his time at Pensacola turned Bill Halsey into the best pilot in the United States Navy, or even into a very good pilot. He made more than his share of bad landings. He ground-looped once and did a front flip another time. Apparently he had the base worried whenever he went into the air. Once, when he could not read the compass because of his bad eyes, he tried following a railroad track, and when the track forked, he followed the wrong branch. It took him quite a while to find his way back to the base, but he made it. Finally, when he could not even see a rope hung with streamers over which he was supposed to fly, he had corrective lenses made and fitted into his goggles.

Before he was through he had flown patrol planes, torpedo planes, and fighter planes—and done a pretty good job of it. His instructor, Bromfield Nichol, then a lieutenant, later said that there was one thing about his flying he could never understand: "The worse the weather, the better he flew."*

But he also won "the Medal of the Benevolent Order of the Flying Jackass." That consisted of an aluminum breastplate cut out in the shape of a jackass, with straps that buckled over the shoulders and around the waist. If a student pilot taxied into a boundary light, he had to wear it, except when flying, until the next student "won" it away from him. Quite early in his student career, Halsey taxied into a boundary light and his plane went on its nose. Whereupon the commanding officer lined up all the students and enlisted men, cleared his throat, and read a citation to Halsey. It went in part:

"In keeping with naval customs and traditions, and the Superintendent of the U.S. Naval Academy's historic phrase 'That in every organization there are certain ones who perform only the duties assigned to them, but there are a few who are ever striving for the greater good and whose efforts and higher attainments set them apart from their fellow men,' it is with the greatest feelings of felicitation and humbuggery that you are cited for the award of the Benevolent Flying Jackass. . . ."

Halsey accepted the "award" in the spirit in which it was given. He wore it for a couple of weeks, then another student hit a boundary light. Halsey refused to give up his medal, however. "When I take command of the *Sara*," he said, "I'm going to put it on the bulkhead of my cabin. If anybody aboard does anything stupid, I'll take a look at the Jackass before I bawl him out, and I'll say, 'Wait a minute, Bill Halsey! You're not so good yourself!' "*

His wife Fan joined him in Pensacola in December. The heat and strain of flying had brought Halsey's weight down from close to 200 to only 155. He was rather proud of his svelte figure. "Pretty good for my age, huh?" he said. She pushed him in front of a mirror, grabbed a handful of the loose skin flapping under his jaw, and demanded, "What are these wattles? You look like a sick turkey buzzard!"*

With that remark in mind, he let some of his missing

poundage return in time to get his wings. And he did get them, in May of 1935, despite age, boundary lights, bad eyes, and the wrong railroad track. Then he and Fan drove across the continent to Long Beach, California, where he would take up his new duties as skipper of the *Saratoga*.

8. "SINK ALL SHIPS ENCOUNTERED"

THE U.S.S. *Saratoga* was the Navy's third carrier. Like the *Langley* and the *Lexington,* it had been started as something else—in this case a battle cruiser. As one of the largest fighting ships in the world, the *Saratoga* was a new experience for a destroyer man. Still Halsey had no trouble. He simply handled her as if she were an overgrown destroyer, which in effect she was. He even tried a destroyer-type "flying anchorage" with her in an emergency—and it worked.

He was captain of the *Saratoga* for two years, and later flew his rear admiral's flag on her for two more. He lived on board her longer than he ever lived anywhere else. Naturally he always had a warm spot in his heart for her.

As commander of the *Saratoga,* Halsey's chief problems involved flying and learning to understand the problems of carrier pilots. Much of this he learned by flying himself. Although he did not attempt to pilot a carrier plane, he rode as a passenger enough times to learn the hazards that face a carrier pilot and the great ability it requires to become a good one.

Whenever he could he continued to pilot planes himself. Before he left the *Sara*, his age, his bad eyes and loss of hearing had resulted in orders that he must be accompanied on all flights by a co-pilot. But that did not keep him out of the air. He had logged more than 1,100 hours before the Japanese attack on Pearl Harbor, and continued to pilot planes, accompanied by a co-pilot, as late as June 1943, when he was a four-star admiral and Commander, South Pacific.

This did not please his wife, and Fan never hesitated to tell him so. When he was relieved from command of the *Sara* with orders to return East, he telephoned her in Wilmington, Delaware, to say he had a chance to make a quick flight home in a two-seater with a fine aviator as co-pilot. She gave him strict orders to come by train. He flew anyway.

Fortunately for him, Halsey had kept his radio tuned too high during the flight, and when they landed at Washington he was for the moment unable to hear a thing. He telephoned Fan to report his safe arrival, but he got no further. At that point she took over the conversation for several minutes. He gathered that she "was ripping off his skin," but he couldn't hear a word. He said he was never that lucky again.*

That was in June of 1937. Halsey's new orders sent him to Pensacola as commandant of the Naval Air Station. Here he could fly as much as he wanted to.

More important, it gave him a chance to learn the latest developments in aviation, and particularly the progress of instrument flying. He took up so much of the instructors' time with his questions, he recalled later, that they finally asked him "to slack off for the benefit of their regular students."* Nevertheless, he continued to prepare himself in every possible way for the air war that was soon to come.

While at Pensacola Halsey received a promotion to rear admiral. In June 1938 he was ordered to sea again—this time as Commander, Carrier Division Two, Aircraft, Battle Force, which consisted of two new carriers, the *Yorktown* and the *Enterprise*. Admiral Halsey hoisted his flag on the *Enterprise*. The "Big E" would be his flagship again through some stirring months to come, and in time would become his favorite ship.

In January 1939 he went with his two carriers to the Caribbean to join the Battle Fleet for spring maneuvers. The Navy now had five carriers, one of which, the *Saratoga,* was in the Pacific. The *Lexington* and *Ranger* made up Carrier Division One, and all four were under the command of Vice Admiral Ernest King, Commander Aircraft, Battle Force.

One morning during the maneuvers, a young officer on the hangar deck of the *Enterprise* made a mistake that delayed the launching of her planes. Immediately a sizzling signal came over from Admiral King demanding to know who was responsible for the delay. Without hesitation Halsey signaled back, "Commander Carrier Division Two."

King had a reputation for toughness in the fleet.

Halsey knew that if he gave the young officer's name, the man would be in for real trouble. He judged the mistake to be due to inexperience and not deserving of that kind of trouble, so he assumed the responsibility himself.

The action was typical of him. No doubt he himself read the young officer out in no uncertain terms, but it did not go beyond that. He believed any man was entitled to one honest mistake; if it went beyond that, Halsey would get the man out of his command. It was no wonder Halsey won the loyalty of his men.

Things moved rapidly for Rear Admiral Halsey. The fleet stopped briefly at Hampton Roads, Virginia, planning to go on to New York for leave and liberty. Halsey was driving his car through Norfolk when an excited yeoman from his staff stopped his car and told him they had been ordered to sail for the West Coast at once. They sailed the next day. Later Halsey learned that the orders had come direct from the White House, which had a report that the Japanese were plotting to blow up the Panama Canal around July 1.

Tension had lessened somewhat by the time they reached the West Coast, but Halsey observed Japanese freighters loading scrap iron at Long Beach and tankers taking on oil. To anyone who had followed the course of events in the Pacific for the past thirty years, the meaning was obvious. Japan was on the march.

It was now a world power, with a sizable army and a powerful navy. In 1931 and 1932 the Japanese seized Manchuria from China on a flimsy pretext.

From 1937 on they were fighting another undeclared war with China in which they succeeded in getting control of most of the port cities and coastal areas.

When the League of Nations protested the aggression, Japan withdrew from the League. When the United States protested and demanded protection of American property in East Asia, the Japanese all but ignored the protests. The stage was set for war, particularly now that the military was in control of the Japanese government with an avowed policy of aggression and expansion.

These things were in Admiral Halsey's mind as he went through maneuvers in the Pacific in 1939 and 1940. In his own way he began to prepare for war as best he could. When war games were held with the Army and one unit of the Army Air Force, 200 miles inland in Nevada, did not bother to post patrols because of the distance, Halsey sent his planes from the *Saratoga* and treated them to a simulated bombing attack. Some of the pilots even dropped alarm clocks by parachute, advising the Army that it was time to wake up.

When in April 1940 the Battle Fleet cruised to the Hawaiian Islands, Halsey spent all the time he could improving means of communication between ships and planes. He thought that by now he had some idea of how naval aviation should be used. Not every officer agreed with his ideas, but he had a way of winning arguments—chiefly because he knew what he was talking about.

Evidently most of his superiors thought so. In

June he was made Commander Aircraft, Battle Force of the Pacific Fleet, with additional duty as Commander, Carrier Division Two. He also received a promotion to vice admiral. This put him only one step from the top of the ladder. The promotion was called temporary, to be sure, but it would prove to be permanent.

That summer he and the rest of the men in the fleet saw a weird contraption on the battleship *California,* just back from the West Coast. It looked something like a bedspring. It was a new and top-secret invention, and it was called radar. Halsey had already heard of it, and was anxious to get it on the *Yorktown,* his new flagship. He soon had it, and put it to work at once. He was amazed to find that it could locate ships 35,000 yards, more than seventeen sea miles, away over the horizon. Later he called radar one of the instruments most important in winning the war in the Pacific, second only to submarines, with planes and bulldozers ranking third and fourth.

In the autumn he took the *Yorktown* back to San Diego for overhaul, and left her there in January to return to Pearl Harbor in the *Enterprise* as his flagship. In January 1941 war with Japan seemed inevitable to many in the Navy. There was also a likelihood that America would become involved in the war which had already been going on in Europe for more than a year. But as far as the Pacific Fleet was concerned, the threat was Japan.

It could not do a great deal to prepare, for it had neither enough ships nor enough men. By 1941, Japan had nine aircraft carriers in commission. The United

States had three in the Pacific, and those were without their full quota of planes. Eventually the Navy was authorized to expand, but at first the result was that trained men had to be taken back from the Pacific to be used in training and leading new groups. Recruits replaced these men, so that as much as seventy per-cent of the men aboard ships in the Pacific Fleet had never heard a gun fired.

In February Rear Admiral Husband E. Kimmel, a classmate of Halsey's, was made Commander in Chief of the Pacific Fleet, with the rank of admiral. Finding that he did not have enough planes, men and ships to maintain an adequate search against possible attack by air or submarines, he was forced to limit the area of search. Yet such a search was necessary in order to protect against a surprise attack. And this seemed likely since the Japanese had attacked both China and Russia before declaring war.

Most military men believed, however, that if Japan struck it would first be to the southward against the Malay Peninsula. If Pearl Harbor were struck first, they thought it would be by submarine, combined with sabotage by the thousands of Japanese who lived in Hawaii. Thus the fleet was anchored at Pearl Harbor, where it would be reasonably secure against submarine attack. Kimmel organized it into three task forces and tried to keep only one task force in port at a time. Halsey was put in command of Task Force 2. Kimmel also, in April 1941, ordered the fleet stripped of all inflammable gear not needed for fighting, and in other ways better prepared for war. He stepped up war-training exercises.

On November 27, 1941, the armed forces in Hawaii received a warning from Washington that war was expected. Japanese envoys were at that time meeting in Washington with American officials to discuss peace, but the United States had broken the Japanese secret code, and had intercepted messages indicating that an attack was coming, though it was impossible to tell where it would be made. That morning a conference was called in Kimmel's office, with Lieutenant General Walter C. Short, Army commander of Hawaii, and members of his staff also present.

Kimmel was troubled about the outer islands—Midway, Wake, Johnston and Palmyra—which were poorly armed and manned. He had sent all the reinforcements he could spare, and new airfields had been built on Wake and Midway. The Army and Navy had agreed to stock them with Army pursuit planes. The *Enterprise* would deliver the planes to Wake, while another task force took planes to Midway. General Short suggested sending the best pursuit planes the Army Air Force had.

Halsey turned to Short's Air Force commander. "Isn't it a fact," he asked, "that your pursuit flyers are forbidden to venture more than fifteen miles from shore?"

He nodded. "That is true."

"Then," Halsey said, "they are no good for our purpose. We need pilots who can navigate over water."*

It was therefore decided to take Marine planes. Halsey stayed on with Kimmel the rest of the day, discussing the project with him. It had to be carried out with absolute secrecy, so that no Japanese spy in Hawaii could learn of it. In the end only the commanding officer of Marine Fighting Squadron 211 was informed. He had to tell his pilots that they were going aboard the *Enterprise* for two days' experimental work. Thus they went aboard with nothing but overnight kits and the clothes they were wearing. Those who survived would get nothing better for a long time to come, for ahead of them lay nearly four years in Japanese prison camps.

Convinced that trouble lay ahead, Halsey asked Kimmel before the task force sailed, "How far do you want me to go?"

"Use your common sense," Kimmel answered.*

That satisfied Halsey. It meant that, as the commander on the scene, he had the authority to act as the situation demanded, whatever that might be. He knew that Kimmel would back him all the way in any action he took. Accordingly, as soon as the task force was beyond signal distance of Pearl Harbor, he issued Battle Order No. 1, which read in part:

"1. The *Enterprise* is now operating under war conditions.

"2. At any time, day or night, we must be ready for instant action.

"3. Hostile submarines may be encountered. . . ."*

He also ordered that warheads be placed on all torpedoes and that all planes be armed with bombs or torpedoes and their full allowance of ammunition. Furthermore, he ordered that pilots were to sink any shipping sighted and shoot down any plane encountered. He had been told there would be no American or Allied shipping in those waters.

His operations officer, who did not know their destination, rushed back to him with the order.

"Admiral," he said unbelievingly, "did you authorize this thing?"

"Yes."

"Do you realize that this means war?"

"Yes."

"Admiral! You can't start a private war of your own! Who's going to take the responsibility?"

"I'll take it!" Halsey answered.*

9. WAR BEGINS

HALSEY FELT completely justified in giving the order. He did not seriously expect to encounter any Japanese warships since nearly everyone believed they were bound south, not east. If he did meet any, however, he was certain they would be on their way to launch a sneak attack and he intended to get in the first blow.

Furthermore, Halsey's mission was secret. He did not want to let any Japanese snooper plane discover his force. Accordingly, he ordered complete radio silence, an antisubmarine patrol, and a morning and evening search of the ocean for 300 miles around.

The force encountered no trouble. On the morning of December 4 the carriers launched the Marine planes about 200 miles from Wake Island and turned back toward Pearl Harbor.

The force planned to arrive at 7:30 A.M. December 7, but it was delayed. Heavy seas kept the destroyers from refueling, and on that morning they were still 200 miles at sea. At six A.M. Halsey sent eighteen of the *Enterprise* planes ahead to land on Ford Island, the naval air station. Then he went below to relax.

He shaved, bathed, put on a clean uniform, and joined his flag secretary, Lieutenant Douglas Moulton, at breakfast. They were drinking a second cup of coffee when the telephone range. Moulton answered it.

"Moulton. . . . *What?* . . . Roger!" He turned to Halsey. "Admiral, the staff duty officer says he has a message that there's an air raid on Pearl!"

"They're shooting at my own boys!" Halsey cried, leaping to his feet. "Tell Kimmel!" *

He had not notified Pearl to expect the Marine planes. He was sure that some trigger-happy gunners had failed to recognize them. He was frantic. But just then his communications officer came in and handed him a dispatch. It read:

From: CINCPAC (Commander in Chief, Pacific Fleet):
To: All ships present
AIR RAID ON PEARL HARBOR X THIS IS NO DRILL.

All hands were notified over the loudspeaker and the ship went to general quarters. Other messages that the Japanese were attacking followed in rapid succession. Then orders came from Kimmel to Task Forces 3, 8 and 12:

RENDEZVOUS AS COMMANDER TASK FORCE 8 DIRECTS X
FURTHER INSTRUCTIONS WHEN ENEMY LOCATED.*

Task Force 3, made up of the heavy cruiser *Indianapolis* and a few destroyers, was then near Johnston Island. Task Force 12 included the carrier *Lexington* and some cruisers and destroyers; it was on its way to put Marine fighter planes on Midway. Shortly thereafter, all available ships at Pearl Harbor were ordered to put to sea, form Task Force 2, and report to Halsey. This gave him operational command of every ship at sea. Though he did not know it, it actually gave him command of what was left of the entire Pacific Fleet.

The next few hours were filled with false rumors and confusion. While Halsey's force waited about 150 miles west of Pearl Harbor for the other task forces to join them, a destroyer steamed by, headed west at top speed. Halsey signaled, "Where are you headed?"

"Don't know," the destroyer answered. "My orders are to steam west at top speed."*

Halsey ordered her to join up . If he hadn't intercepted her, she seemed bound to end up on the coast of China.

Halsey sent word to Kimmel that he was depending upon him for scouting information. Half his own scouting planes had already been flown into Pearl, and some were shot down in the confusion by American gunners. The rest he would need if he found the enemy.

Meanwhile, he hoisted his battle flags. A dispatch came advising him that the enemy was off to the southwest, so he formed up the now combined task forces and headed in that direction, ordering the ships to search and fire on contact. They found nothing.

The next dispatch advised that a Japanese carrier was south of Pearl. Halsey launched what he had left— 21 planes of Torpedo Squadron 6, accompanied by 6 smoke planes for camouflage and 6 fighters. They also found nothing. The torpedo and smoke planes, the former still loaded with torpedoes carrying warheads, managed to land safely at night on the deck of the *Enterprise*, despite their pilots being untrained in night landings. The 6 fighters went on to Pearl, and 4 were shot down by American antiaircraft guns, although the base had been notified of their return.

That night Halsey paced the deck in a rage, waiting for some word of the location of the Japanese that would be more than rumor, but it never came. He was not sure what he could do even if he met the Japanese, for he had nothing but cruisers to oppose battleships, and his few planes could have done little damage. Still, he would have made a fight of it, hoping to keep the enemy busy until the *Lexington*'s task force arrived with more planes. This chasing about blindly was not easy for him to take.

Actually, the launching point of the Japanese planes had been some 200 miles north of Oahu, but Halsey would not learn this until later, when Intelligence had been able to examine charts found on the bodies of downed Japanese carrier pilots.

On the following day, low on fuel, Halsey took the *Enterprise* and seven destroyers back to Pearl. They steamed into the harbor at dusk, and for the first time he saw with his own eyes what had happened. Four American battleships and 2 lesser ships had been sunk at their berths, while 4 more battleships, 3 cruisers, 3 destroyers and 2 other ships had been damaged, and 188 Navy and Army aircraft destroyed. More than 2,000 men—Army, Navy and Marine Corps—had been killed and more than 1,000 wounded. All this had cost the Japanese 5 midget submarines, 28 planes, and fewer than 100 men.

The target ship *Utah* lay sunk at her berth in the harbor. This was the berth the *Enterprise* would have occupied had she not been delayed by the heavy seas.

For some time Halsey said nothing, but only looked at the wreckage. Then he spoke. "Before we're through with 'em, the Japanese language will be spoken only in hell!"* His violent hatred of the Japanese continued throughout the war and afterward.

Wild rumors abounded at Pearl Harbor: Eight Japanese transports had been seen rounding Barbers Point. Japanese gliders and paratroopers had just landed at Kaneohe. An enemy carrier was reported operating off California.

There was no truth in any of these reports, but they persisted. Some of the hysteria was even carried to sea, perhaps largely because there were so many inexperienced young officers and men in the fleet. When Halsey sailed out with his task force next day to look for Japanese submarines which Intelligence believed were in the area, he found his lookouts spying periscopes in every whitecap and torpedoes in every porpoise.

One destroyer did make an apparent submarine contact and started on its track. A young officer watched her from the bridge of the *Enterprise*.

Suddenly he shouted, "Look! She's sinking! There she goes!"*

Halsey put his glasses on her. The destroyer's hull had simply dropped out of sight in a trough of the waves. She rode up on the next crest. By now even Halsey's nerves were getting a little raw.

"If you ever make another report like that, sir," he told the young officer, "I'll throw you over the side!"*

As the day wore on, the jitters of the lookouts grew worse. Finally Halsey sent this message to the entire task force:

IF ALL THE TORPEDO WAKES ARE FACTUAL, JAPANESE SUBMARINES WILL SOON HAVE TO RETURN TO BASE FOR A RELOAD, AND WE WILL HAVE NOTHING TO FEAR X IN ADDITION, WE ARE WASTING TOO MANY DEPTH CHARGES ON NEUTRAL FISH X TAKE ACTION ACCORDINGLY.*

In the next few days patrol planes actually did sight three enemy submarines and damaged at least one.

After the war, a Congressional investigating committee recommended a reprimand to Admiral Kimmel and General Short, for the Pearl Harbor disaster, thus in effect putting an end to their military careers. Halsey felt this was unjustified. In his autobiography he said:

". . . the attack succeeded because Admiral Kimmel and General Short could not give Pearl Harbor adequate protection. They could not give it because Congress would not authorize it. Congress is elected by the American people. And the blame for Pearl

Harbor rests squarely on the American people and nowhere else. Instead of trying to dodge our responsibility by smirching two splendid officers, we should be big enough to acknowledge our mistakes—and wise enough to profit by them."*

10. "HAUL OUT WITH HALSEY"

THE JAPANESE moved on as if invincible. They occupied Guam and Wake islands and invaded the Philippines. They landed in Borneo and occupied the capital of Thailand. They seized Hong Kong from the British and sank two British ships, a battleship and a cruiser, off Malaya. Everywhere they overwhelmed forces that were weak or ill prepared for war, and the majority of the Japanese began to believe that they were indeed invincible.

Many Japanese naval officers were not so sure. They shared the dislike of the United States felt by most of their countrymen. They were angry that America and Great Britain had opposed their expansion in Asia and the Pacific. Crowded as the Japanese were on their little islands, they felt that they deserved room to grow like other nations. Being Asians, they thought that Asia should be theirs to exploit. They were also furious that, at the naval disarmament conferences of 1921 and 1930, Great Britain and the United States had refused to agree to let them build enough warships to hold their own, at least defensively, against the fleets of the other two nations. Japan too considered itself a world power now, as indeed it was.

What had most disturbed the Japanese Navy was the oil embargo placed upon them in July 1941 after Japanese forces moved into southern Indochina. After that Britain, the United States and the Netherlands would sell them no more oil. And after that, the Navy strategists realized that they must strike quickly or not at all. They did not have enough oil to last out a long war.

That was what caused them, after some debate, to decide upon the attack on Pearl Harbor. If they could disable most of the American fleet, they would have time to complete their Asian conquests and get oil from Indonesia before the United States could put together a new fleet strong enough to attack them.

But the success of the surprise attack, the Navy strategists believed, depended upon sinking or damaging the American carriers. They had thought that there were four carriers based at Pearl Harbor. They found none. Thus the battle had to them been a failure. They wanted to strike again, to hunt down the American carriers and sink them. But the imperial staff would not allow it on the grounds that the fleet was needed elsewhere, in operations near the mainland of Asia.

These things, of course, no American knew at the time. All Halsey knew was that the Japanese had dealt American forces a crippling blow at Pearl Harbor and that the U.S. Navy had been unable to strike back. This was very much on his mind on January 9, 1942, when he sat down across the desk from the newly appointed Commander-in-Chief, Pacific Fleet, Admiral Chester W. Nimitz, thenceforth to be known officially as CINCPAC. Soon after Pearl Harbor Admiral Kimmel had asked to be relieved, and Nimitz was his replacement. Halsey had known him since Annapolis days when he was two classes behind Halsey. Now Nimitz outranked him.

"You sent for me, Chester," Halsey said.

"I did." CINCPAC wasted no time in getting down to business. He explained that the Japanese had just seized the British Gilbert Islands and it looked as if Samoa would be next. That would put them directly across the American line of communications with New Zealand and Australia. "Unless," he said, "we hit them hard and fast. We're not ready to hit them anywhere with an amphibious landing."

"So," Halsey said, "it's up to the carrier task forces."

Nimitz nodded. Rear Admiral Frank Jack Fletcher, he explained, was now escorting Marine reinforcements to Samoa with Task Force 17, which included the *Yorktown*. What he had in mind was for Halsey to join Fletcher at Samoa with his Task Force 8, then lead both forces in a strike against the Marshall and Gilbert islands.

"How does that sound?" Nimitz asked. "It's a rare opportunity."*

Halsey took a deep breath. Ever since he had sailed into Pearl Harbor and seen the wreckage there, he had been filled with a mighty rage and an itch to hit back. Nonetheless, this could be a rough one. There was no way of knowing what he would be facing. The Marshalls had been under Japanese control since World War I. The Japanese were not supposed to fortify them, but probably they had, with both airfields and submarine bases. No one could be sure because no one except Japanese had been allowed on or near the islands for years.

Halsey hesitated only an instant. "I'm ready," he said.

At times in the next three weeks Halsey wondered if he had not spoken too soon. From the very beginning bad luck seemed to dog the operation. Just before they left Pearl Harbor, on January 11, word came to him that the *Saratoga* had been torpedoed and would have to go into drydock. That left only three carriers in the Pacific—the *Enterprise, Yorktown* and *Lexington*—of which the first two would be putting themselves in danger on this operation. On the thirteenth, a scout pilot forgot himself and broke radio silence, thus endangering the whole operation.

"I might have known it," the Admiral growled to his chief of staff. "The thirteenth."

Commander Miles Browning allowed the faintest flicker of a smile to cross his harsh face. He knew about the Admiral's superstition, resulting from that gun turret explosion on the *Missouri*.

The next day one of the destroyers lost a man overboard. Two days later a sailor was killed in a gun turret accident and a scout plane crashed on the deck of the *Enterprise*, killing a machinist's mate. The same day, one of her torpedo planes failed to return. What bothered the Admiral most of all was that he could not search the area thoroughly to determine whether the crew had gotten into a raft. This was war, and the task force had to sail on.

He was still troubled about this thirty-four days later when word came that all three of the crew had drifted 750 miles on a rubber raft and arrived safely at Pukapuka Island. After decorating them, his first words to the pilot were:

"Are you still speaking to me, after the way I had to go off and leave you?"

"Yes, sir," the pilot replied. "I knew what you were up against."*

The following day, an *Enterprise* scout plane crashed into the water, killing the radioman and crippling the pilot. Three days later a torpedo plane scored a direct hit on a Japanese submarine, but the bomb failed to explode and the submarine went on its way. Halsey did not know then that there would be more such incidents, that many of our bombs and torpedoes were poorly made and would fail to explode.

On January 22, two destroyers collided in a heavy rain and had to go back to Pearl Harbor.

And so it went. The task force sailed on, but on the flag (admiral's) bridge the bulldog jaws of Admiral Halsey tightened with increasing strain. There was too much at stake for him to feel otherwise. The war would not be won if this operation were a success, but it could be all but lost if it were a failure.

As they neared the islands, Halsey divided Task

Force 8 into three groups, each to strike at different islands, the cruisers and destroyers with ship-to-shore bombardment, the *Enterprise* with her planes. Fletcher, with his smaller force, would be hitting the more southerly islands of the chain. The attack was set for February 1.

On the afternoon of the day before the radarman called out, "Bogey at two six zero!"

Halsey crouched over the screen, looked at the gray spot that meant an approaching Japanese patrol plane. The Japanese pilot was within forty miles now. Surely he would spot the fleet at any instant. They would hear the crackle of his radio, sending word back to the Japanese base. Not only would their hope of a surprise attack be lost, but they would be open to daylight attack by torpedo and bomber planes, with the *Enterprise* the prime target.

The distance lessened to thirty-eight miles. Still there was no warning sound on the radio. The moving gray spot was now within thirty-four miles, and the Admiral held his breath.

Then he saw that the distance had begun to increase. The patrol plane was going on its way, and had sounded no warning!

"He didn't see us," Halsey said. "The haze must have hidden us."

At once he called for his Japanese language officer. "Translate this message," he said. " 'From the American admiral in charge of the striking force, to the Japanese admiral on the Marshall Islands: It is a pleasure to thank you for having your patrol plane not sight my force.' "*

He smiled, but the smile was grim. "Tomorrow, while they're bombing, we'll have all our planes drop copies of this." Knowing the Japanese, he knew that tomorrow night there would be one less Japanese patrol plane pilot.

That night proved clear and calm. The ships fueled in the open sea without trouble. Things began to look better. Still Halsey was nervous. He went to his cabin but could not sleep. So many things could go wrong. The charts were old and probably inaccurate. There could be reefs to run aground upon which did not show on the charts. There could be minefields. And any crippled ship would be a sitting duck for the Japanese planes.

At 4:43 A.M., under a full moon, he sent the first planes roaring off the *Enterprise*. Nine torpedo planes took off for Kwajalein and thirty-seven dive bombers for Roi. Six fighters, known as CAP (combat air patrol) went up to protect the carrier herself. Behind them the carrier and her protecting ships were left to wait, and the Admiral to worry, until the planes came back. The ships cruised about on a meandering course, already planned in advance, so that their own planes would be able to find them and the Japanese would find it hard to do so.

On the flag bridge Halsey had his earphones on, waiting for the moment the attack began and the pilots could break radio silence. He had a long time to wait, pacing the bridge and looking out to the dark horizon. The strike was timed at Roi for 6:58, but it did not come. At 7:06 A.M. he heard the sound of the first bomb of the war to strike Japanese territory.

Immediately thereafter the American planes were in trouble. They had been delayed by poor charts and by mist and darkness, and that gave the Japanese time to be ready, with AA (antiaircraft fire) and with fighter planes in the air. The plane that dropped the first bomb was shot down, as well as three others. But the returning pilots believed they had destroyed ten Japanese planes, two big hangars, an ammunition dump, a fuel depot, and the radio building.

At Kwajalein, Halsey could tell, the going was better. There was heavy AA, but no fighter interception. The planes also found lots of shipping to hit, so much so that after a few minutes the strike leader came on the air. They could use more bombers, he said. "You'll get 'em," the Admiral assured him. He sent nine more torpedo planes off the *Enterprise,* rerouted some of the bombers from Roi.

Awhile later he could hear their pilots talking. "Get away from that cruiser, Jack! She's mine!" and, "Bingo!" and "Look at that big one burn!"*

This time the Admiral himself counted the planes as they came back to land and refuel. Every one of them returned safely. The pilots reported an estimate of two submarines sunk, one light cruiser, a small carrier, and four other ships sunk or severely damaged, two patrol planes destroyed on the water, and a large compound shattered by three direct hits.

Meanwhile cruisers and destroyers were bombarding Taroa and Wotje islands while *Enterprise* fighter planes protected them in the air.

Altogether that day the *Enterprise* launched and

landed planes twenty-one times. Lieutenant Commander William R. Hollingsworth, skipper of Bombing Squadron 6, led three of these strikes. He came back from the third around one o'clock in the afternoon and reported to the bridge. Then he said, "Admiral, don't you think it's about time we got out of here?"*

Halsey looked over at Wotje Island, so close that with his naked eye he could see its AA bursting around the *Enterprise* planes, and also see a column of smoke rising from the burning installations. For nine hours his ship had been maneuvering in a rectangle only five miles by twenty, close to shore. So far she had been lucky, but once she had dodged a periscope, and sooner or later enemy planes were bound to find her.

The Admiral nodded. "My boy," he said, "I've been thinking the same thing myself!"*

He passed the word to get going, and that was the beginning of a club known for the rest of the war as "Haul out with Halsey."

The order came a little late. They were on their way, heading northwestward half an hour later, when Halsey saw five twin-engine Japanese bombers come out of the overcast and glide down toward the starboard bow of the *Enterprise*. He could see the bomb bays open and distinguish each separate bomb as it dropped.

With over forty years at sea and one world war behind him, it was the first time Admiral Halsey had ever been directly under attack. But his reactions were that of any sane fighting man. Before Miles

Browning yelled "Down!" Halsey was flat on the deck of the bridge. He claimed afterward that he was the first one down, and that the footprints of most of the other men on the bridge were on his back.

He felt the deck shake beneath him as the bombs exploded, so close together that he could not count them. There were fifteen in all, but all fell into the water. One came so close, though, that it riddled the side of the ship, caused a small fire, and killed one sailor.

The Admiral got to his feet, still wearing the white sun helmet that his staff had wanted him to swap for one that was not such a target. He was scared, he said afterward, but more angry than scared. He was up in time to see one of the Japanese planes slide out of the formation and turn back toward the ship. Both its engines were on fire, but the pilot was making a perfect approach up the groove. He intended to crash among the planes parked on the forward end of the flight deck. It was a suicide run, but not in the sense of the *kamikaze* attacks that were to come later in the war, for this pilot knew he could not have made it back to base.

A young sailor jumped into the seat of the rearmost plane and opened fire. The captain of the *Enterprise* ordered helm hard over. The Japanese pilot could not correct his course. He slashed the tail off the plane where the sailor was crouched, hit the flight deck and toppled into the water.

The Admiral took a deep breath and stepped into flag plot for a steadying cup of coffee. As he drank it, he happened to look up and catch the yeoman of the day grinning at him.

"What are you laughing at?" he asked.

The yeoman flushed. "Nothing, sir," he mumbled.

"Who is this man?" the Admiral asked Miles Browning.

"Why, Admiral," Browning said, puzzled, "that's Bowman. He's on your staff."

"I don't mean that. What's his rate?"

"Yeoman first class, sir."

"That's where you're wrong," Halsey said. "He's a *chief* yeoman. Any man who can grin like that while my knees are cracking together deserves to be promoted."*

Ira N. Bowman ended the war a senior lieutenant. Actually, if we are to believe those members of the Admiral's staff who saw Halsey many times under fire, he was not as nervous as he claimed to be. Before an action he worried constantly, but once the shooting started he was cool and quiet. This incident does serve to show his awareness of and concern for every man who served under him. He never forgot, when the planes took off from the flight deck, that he was sending some men out to die. He was so proud of them all that he would have liked to promote and decorate every man in the fleet. Which was one reason why just about every man in the fleet was proud to serve under Halsey.

Two hours later, with the task force reformed and steaming at thirty knots, they were attacked again by two Japanese bombers. This time the bombs did not even come close, and both planes were brought down, one by AA fire and one by fighter planes. Japanese planes followed them the rest of the afternoon, but did not attack. Probably, Halsey reasoned, the Japanese were waiting for darkness. The night promised to be clear, and they would have easier pickings. He turned to Commander Browning. It was time to fool them, he said.

"What do you have in mind, sir?" Browning asked.

"They know we're heading back for Pearl. They expect us to continue on course. We'll change course."

He ordered the task force to swing 100 degrees to port, away from Pearl Harbor. They followed that course for several hours, then headed again for Pearl. The Japanese planes did not find them again.

Five days later Task Force 8 steamed into Pearl Harbor with their largest flags flying. The roar that went up must have been heard all the way across the island of Oahu. The ships in the harbor blew their sirens and the crews yelled. The troops at Hickam Field and the wounded patients at Hospital Point cheered them all the way back to their mooring. The men of the task force tried to cheer back but choked up.

"I myself cried," the Admiral said, "and was not ashamed."*

As would prove true so often during the war, the raid had not done as much damage as the American pilots believed at the time. Nevertheless, a check with Japanese records after the war showed that two small Japanese ships were sunk and eight others, including a cruiser, damaged. Thirteen planes were destroyed and five others badly damaged. In addition, Rear Admiral Yashiro, the Marshall Islands area commander, and about ninety other Japanese were killed. It had not been a great victory, but it had been an important one. For the first time since Pearl Harbor the U.S. Pacific Fleet, crippled as it was, had struck back at the enemy—and struck them when they least expected it. There was still a long way to go, with many dark days ahead, but they were on the way.

Admiral Halsey was given the Distinguished Service Medal "for his brilliant and audacious attack against the Marshall and Gilbert Islands."

11. BOMBS AWAY OVER TOKYO

MORE RAIDS on Japanese-held islands by Halsey's task force soon followed the attack on the Gilbert-Marshall islands. The first was upon Wake Island.

The task force was originally designated Number 13, and scheduled to leave Pearl Harbor on Friday, February 13. Bearing in mind Halsey's feelings about the number thirteen, his chief of staff protested to CINCPAC headquarters. The group was changed to Task Force 16 and the date of departure to the fourteenth. It was practically the same group as the former Task Force 8, including the *Enterprise*, two heavy cruisers and half a dozen destroyers. The cruisers and two destroyers were to serve as a bombardment group, approaching from the west, while the *Enterprise*, protected by her destroyers, launched her planes from the north.

Bad weather delayed the strike, but it was finally

executed, with some seaplanes and small craft destroyed, and damage done to shore installations. They were retiring from the attack when a message came from CINCPAC:

DESIRABLE TO STRIKE MARCUS IF YOU THINK IT FEASIBLE.*

Marcus Island was a Japanese base only 999 miles from Tokyo. Supposedly well defended, it lay within easy flying range of the Japanese air base at Iwo Jima. This could be a mean one. Nevertheless Halsey, as Nimitz no doubt expected, thought the raid "feasible."

The next morning the task force reformed and Halsey set the course for 275 degrees True, or almost due west. From time to time he heard his staff officers muttering, as they passed the compass: "Two-seven-five . . . Two-seven-five . . . Why do we always seem to retire to the westward?"*

They caught the Japanese completely by surprise at Marcus. When the first bombs struck, the Japanese radio started to sound an alert, but was promptly knocked off the air by a direct hit. A plane flew over from Iwo to investigate. The report it sent back caused an alert and a blackout in Tokyo. One American plane was lost to antiaircraft fire, but the rest of the task force made it safely back to Pearl Harbor.

Not much damage was done at Marcus Island, but there was not much there to be damaged. This raid, like the one on Wake Island, was made primarily to worry and disconcert the Japanese. By this time they controlled all land and sea between the Solomon

Islands and Burma and China, as well as everything north of Australia, except for Bataan and the south coast of New Guinea. Bataan would soon fall, and Port Moresby in New Guinea was next on their list. If Port Moresby fell, a good part of the populated area of Australia would be within bombing range. It was hoped that these raids near the homeland would cause the Japanese to slow down their drive to the southwest, perhaps even delay it until the United States had enough ships and men in the area to stop them. The United States had committed itself to defending the entire Pacific, since Great Britain and her other allies had their hands more than full in the European theater of war. Furthermore, American ships and men and supplies were needed there, too, so that America at best could fight only a defensive war in the Pacific at this stage.

Halsey had been back from the Marcus raid only a few days when he and Miles Browning were called in to CINCPAC headquarters again for a conference with an admiral from Commander-in-Chief Ernest King's office in Washington. This time something really big was coming up—big, at least, from the standpoint of danger involved. Lieutenant Colonel James Doolittle had, with Navy cooperation, been training sixteen Army Air Force crews to take B-25 bombers off the deck of a carrier. The Navy had agreed to launch them for Tokyo!

"Do you believe it would work, Bill?" Nimitz asked Halsey.

"They'll need a lot of luck," Halsey answered. "Are you willing to take them out there?"

"Yes, I am."

"Good!" Nimitz said. "It's all yours!"*

Halsey and Browning flew to San Francisco to talk things over with Doolittle, who was waiting there for the B-25s to arrive. Halsey told him they would carry his planes within 400 miles of Tokyo—if they were not discovered. If Japanese ships or planes sighted them before that, they would have to launch sooner, since they could not risk the loss of the carriers. In any case, they would launch within reach of either Tokyo or Midway. Doolittle agreed to that, and they shook hands on it.

There would be two task forces involved in the operation, 16 and 18. The planes were put aboard the newest American carrier, the *Hornet,* at the Alameda Air Base and stowed on the flight deck. Since the *Hornet* would therefore be unable to protect itself against enemy air attack, the *Enterprise* must provide the necessary air cover. Captain Marc Mitscher commanded the *Hornet,* while Halsey would remain on his flagship in command of the entire operation. He was also given a new title, which he would keep until he got a bigger one the following October: Commander Carriers Pacific Fleet, with additional duty as COMCARDIV Two.

Halsey and Browning flew back to Pearl Harbor, the Admiral having left directions for the *Hornet* and the rest of Task Force 18 to join up with the *Enterprise* task force at a point about halfway between Kamchatka and Pearl. Although well on the way to Tokyo, this spot should be out of range of Japanese search planes, and so an unlikely place to be discovered.

They rendezvoused at the appointed time. Until then no man aboard the *Enterprise*, except for Halsey and Browning, knew their destination. Halsey felt that there was no longer any danger that one of the ships might become disabled, have to go back to Pearl, and let the word out. So he announced over the loudspeaker:

"This force is bound for Tokyo."*

Cheers roared through the gangways and up to the flight deck of the *Enterprise*.

On April 17, 1942, the carriers and cruisers were fueled at sea, 1,000 miles east of Tokyo. Then the destroyers and tankers were left behind and the bigger ships went on alone. This did not give them the best of protection against submarines, but Halsey had found it wise policy on the Marcus Island raid. There the light destroyers could not match the speed of the others in the heavy seas, and the same kind of weather was likely to be encountered just ahead. There were patrol planes to spot any submarines and cruisers to sink them. Halsey never feared to take chances, and more often than not it paid off.

Another situation of a similar sort was coming up, and this time the Admiral made an entirely different choice.

They ran in toward Tokyo at twenty-three knots. All was going well. Then, at three o'clock on the morning of the eighteenth, the ships' radars began to show blips on their screens. Those probably meant enemy picket vessels. Halsey maneuvered the ships well around them, and the task forces were undiscovered. At least, no warning radio crackles sounded.

At 7:45, however, they sighted another vessel about six miles away. Halsey messaged the cruiser *Nashville* to sink it with gunfire. The *Nashville* opened fire, but before the picket vessel went down, the *Enterprise* intercepted a nearby radio transmission. Apparently the picket had gotten the alarm to Tokyo.

They were still more than 650 miles from the capital of Japan. That extra 250 miles could mean the difference between life and death for Doolittle's flyers waiting on the *Hornet*. Doolittle's plan had been to take off alone at 2 P.M. that day and scatter incendiaries over Tokyo, thus lighting up the target area for the rest of his squadron. They would follow a few hours later, arriving after dark. This would give them a better chance, since the Japanese had no radar controls on their antiaircraft guns, and so would be less accurate at night. Halsey felt that the chances of the airmen making a landing after the raid in a friendly airfield in China, 1,100 miles beyond Tokyo, were pretty slim at best. Yet they could not even follow Doolittle's plan if they took off now.

It was not an easy decision, but Halsey made it in less than ten minutes. He had with him two of the only five carriers in the entire Pacific Fleet, and one of the others was still under repair on the West Coast. He was now within bombing range of Japanese planes and well within striking range of Japanese submarines. It added up to sixteen American planes and their crews against half the operational carriers in the Pacific. He could risk those carriers no longer. At eight o'clock he signaled to Captain Mitscher on the *Hornet:*

LAUNCH PLANES X TO COL DOOLITTLE AND HIS GALLANT COMMAND GOOD LUCK AND GOD BLESS YOU.*

Every man on deck in the task force watched and sweated the planes off. The wind and sea were strong, but Jimmy Doolittle took off in spite of it. The rest of the squadron followed swiftly. The B-25s were not designed for carrier takeoffs, and one pilot almost stalled and ended in the sea, but he finally made it—as did the others.

At 9:24 the last of the sixteen was airborne.

Immediately, Halsey ordered: "Commence retirement from the area at twenty-five knots. Course zero nine oh."

They were headed back for Pearl Harbor, but the Japanese picket ship had gotten its warning through. In the next three hours, American patrol planes attacked sixteen Japanese vessels, one a submarine. The *Nashville* sank one ship and picked up four prisoners out of the water. One of them, though wounded, talked willingly. He said he had roused his captain just before dawn to look at some planes. The skipper refused to get out of his bunk. Later the sailor woke him up again and reported, "Two of our beautiful carriers ahead, sir!"

The skipper came on deck and studied them through his glass. "They're beautiful," he said, "but they're not ours." He went below and put a bullet through his head.*

The task force tuned in its radios to Tokyo and listened to a broadcaster describe in English the wonders of life in Japan. Of all the warring countries in the world, he said, Japan was free from enemy attack. Furthermore, its navy would demolish any foe that dared approach its shores. Thus the happy inhabitants could today enjoy the Festival of the Cherry Blossoms.

At that point the listening U.S. Navy men heard the air-raid sirens go on in Tokyo. Doolittle and his men had arrived.

They also got away. Not a single one was shot down over Japan, although two pilots who landed in China were picked up by the Japanese and executed. The Chinese hid most of the others until they could be spirited out, and they eventually made it back home. They had done no great damage, but the results were far-reaching. At the moment the Doolittle raid delayed the Japanese invasion of the Solomons and Port Moresby by a few days, as well as causing them to hold hundreds of planes at home to defend Tokyo. Furthermore, it speeded up their plans to destroy the U.S. Pacific Fleet, and so helped lead to eventual Japanese disaster at the Battle of Midway.

As for Halsey, he was doomed in the next couple of months to two big disappointments. First, he missed the Battle of the Coral Sea. While he was still out with Doolittle, CINCPAC had gotten wind of the Japanese plan to invade Port Moresby and occupy Tulagi in the Solomons. Nimitz had ordered Task Force 17, which included carriers *Lexington* and *Yorktown,* to stop the

Japanese. As soon as Halsey returned from the Tokyo raid, he went barreling down to join the battle. But he arrived too late. At the cost of the *Lexington* and two smaller ships, the Japanese were stopped, with one of their small carriers sunk and two big ones damaged. Halsey was still 1,000 miles away.

Halsey delivered a squadron of Marine fighter planes at Nouméa, New Caledonia, and then turned north. The Japanese forces had disappeared after the battle, and he wanted to make certain the they were not planning to slip between the New Hebrides and the Fijis in another attempt to break the American lifeline to Australia. At that point he received a message from COMINCH (Admiral King) by way of CIN-CPAC, stating that it was "inadvisable for Task Force 16 to operate beyond the coverage of our shore-based air or within range of enemy shore-based air."*

Halsey was furious. At the moment he was doing just what the orders of the Commander-in-Chief forbade him to do, for he was as near to the air base which the Japanese had managed to set up in the Solomons as to the Allied bases at Nouméa and the Fijis. Yet if he did not continue farther north and the Japanese were planning a breakthrough, he would be risking the loss of more American bases.

He kept on going north.

He believed that the man on the spot should have discretion in such matters, since he would know the situation better than could anyone back at Headquarters. From his point of view this made sense, yet he was deliberately disobeying orders. Such disobedience could hardly have endeared Halsey to his superiors, but it seems not to have landed him in trouble. He kept on north until satisfied that the Japanese were planning no breakthrough, then turned back.

The next day he received direct orders from CINCPAC to return to Pearl. Before he could collect his tankers and other scattered ships, another dispatch came in from CINCPAC: EXPEDITE RETURN.

Obviously, trouble was building up somewhere else in the Pacific. Halsey hurried back with his fleet to Pearl, arriving on May 26. What was brewing was the Battle of Midway, with him slated for command of the fleet.

He did not make it. Six months on the bridge, in the tropical sun and under tension, had taken their toll. He came down with a terrible itch, so bad that he could scarcely sleep. The doctors called it "general dermatitis," but it was more popularly known as hives. They ordered him to the hospital.

From the naval hospital, "itching to get into the fight,"* as Admiral Nimitz said, Halsey watched his beloved flattops sortie forth to win the most important carrier battle of the war.

12. COMMANDER SOUTH PACIFIC

THE BATTLE of the Coral Sea had delayed execution of the Japanese grand plan, but by no means caused them to abandon it. In fact, they considered that it had been a victory for them since they believed they had sunk two American carriers and other large ships. Flushed with their many easy victories, they intended now to seize Midway and the Aleutians, Port Moresby and the Solomon Islands, New Caledonia, Fiji and Samoa. With the islands they already held, they would then have a ring of defenses covering most of the Pacific. The lines of communication between the United States and Australia would be cut for good.

After that they would sue for peace with America. They believed that, faced with a long and all but impossible war, the United States would agree to such a peace. Then they would be free to take over what they wanted of Asia and the islands of the Pacific.

In the opinion of such wise strategists as Fleet Admiral Isoroku Yamamoto, however, one thing came first. The U.S. Pacific Fleet must be destroyed. He knew something of American ingenuity and American machinery. If the war continued, by 1943 there would be enough new American fighting ships in the Pacific to make Japanese victory impossible. The time to strike was now, and the place to strike was Midway, with an additional strike at the Aleutians. This, he believed, would draw forth all the U.S. carriers and he could destroy them.

In time Imperial General Headquarters came around to his way of thinking. On May 5, 1942, the order was issued: "Commander in Chief Combined Fleet [Yamamoto] will, in cooperation with the Army, invade and occupy strategic points in the Western Aleutians and Midway Island." Thereafter Yamamoto sortied from Japan with a fleet of 162 ships, including 4 big carriers. (He would have had six if two had not been damaged in the Coral Sea battle.) Against him Nimitz could gather only 76 ships, 3 of them carriers.

In spite of the odds, the Battle of Midway, fought in early June, was a decisive victory for the United States. The Japanese lost all four of their carriers; the Americans lost one, the *Yorktown*. Thanks to the superb planning and performance of Admirals Nimitz, Spruance and Fletcher, and the courage and skill of the airmen who flew under their command, the whole course of the war in the Pacific had been changed in a few days. A long road still lay ahead, and America and her allies still could not spare all the men and materials needed to fight the Pacific war. But in spite of that, they need no longer fight an entirely defensive war.

In fact, the means were already being prepared for the first step on the road to Tokyo. In May details GA-202 and MA-202—bluejackets and Marines —set sail from Norfolk, Virginia, aboard the U.S.S. *Wakefield*, a transport converted from the former luxury liner *Manhattan*. No enlisted man aboard knew their destination, and guesses ranged from Martinique to some barren Pacific island that must be recaptured from the Japanese. They had to be setting up a base somewhere, it seemed, in view of all the radiomen and other technicians in GA-202, the bluejacket contingent. Besides, there was a Marine general named A. Archer Vandegrift aboard.

Twenty-six days later they sailed into the harbor of Wellington, New Zealand, where they were greeted by a band playing "Roll Out the Barrel." The bluejackets went on by train to Auckland, there to help set up the COMSOPAC command—Commander South Pacific—being established under Vice Admiral Robert Ghormley. The Marines stayed for the time being near Wellington, to undergo further training for the amphibious landings at Guadalcanal and Tulagi in the Solomons, slated to take place in August.

While these things were happening, Halsey spent an impatient two months in hospitals in Pearl Harbor and Richmond, Virginia. Finally certified fit for active duty again, and itching now only from a desire to get back into the war, he stayed but a few days with his family in Wilmington. There one of his grandsons, Halsey Spruance, burst excitedly into the room.

"Look, Grandaddy!" he shouted. "You're famous. Here you are in the funny papers!"*

And with that knowledge to keep him stimulated, he reported back to Admiral Nimitz at Pearl early in September. There something happened which pleased him much more than being a comic-book hero. On the twelfth, Admiral Nimitz invited him to a ceremony on the *Saratoga*, where CINCPAC was presenting decorations. With all hands lined up on the flight deck, Nimitz stepped to the microphone, beckoning Halsey forward.

"Boys," Admiral Nimitz said, "I've got a surprise for you. Bill Halsey's back!"*

Cheers roared out. And Bill Halsey, being a sentimental man, found his eyes filling with tears.

He was slated to take command of a carrier task force built around the *Enterprise*, but it was not yet ready. He would be operating in the South Pacific, so while waiting he decided to tour the area and familiarize himself with it, see the bases and talk to the men he would be working with. He also thought he should pay his respects to General Douglas MacArthur, COMSOWESPAC (Commander, Southwest Pacific). On orders from President Roosevelt, MacArthur had left the Philippines before the fall of Bataan and was now welding together, from his headquarters in Brisbane, a force of Australian and American soldiers and flyers to make good his promise that he would return to the Philippines. He also had a small unit of the Navy under his command. While the Combined Chiefs of Staff in Washington had directed that CINCPAC must

exercise *strategic* control of any naval operations anywhere in the Pacific, any naval units operating in Mac-
Arthur's area would be under his *tactical* command—
that is, would take orders from him once an operation
was planned.

In any case, Army and Navy and Marines, Austral-
ians and New Zealanders and Dutch would all be
working together—must all work together if the war
was to be won. It would be wise, as well as courteous,
to talk things over with MacArthur. Halsey thoroughly
believed in the cooperation of all the fighting forces.

As it turned out, he did not get to talk with Mac-
Arthur until some months later. On October 18, as his
Coronado flying boat settled down on Nouméa Harbor,
where Advance Headquarters of COMSOPAC had
been established early in the Guadalcanal campaign,
Lieutenant Commander Wintle, Vice Admiral Ghormley's flag lieutenant, came alonside in a whaleboat
and handed Halsey a sealed envelope. It was a dispatch
from CINCPAC:

YOU WILL TAKE COMMAND OF THE SOUTH PACIFIC AREA
AND SOUTH PACIFIC FORCES IMMEDIATELY.*

The Admiral read the dispatch twice, then swore
the oath he reserved only for special occasions. He
turned to Colonel Julian Brown, his Intelligence officer. "This," he said, "is the hottest potato they ever
handed me!"*

He did not exaggerate. The situation in the South
Pacific was desperate. Although the Marines had made
their landings on Tulagi and Guadalcanal on August 7,
they were now barely hanging on to the ground they had

won. Two days after the landing four cruisers, three American and one Australian, were sunk in a surprise attack by the Japanese off Savo Island. In September the carrier *Wasp* had been torpedoed near Espiritu Santo. Five destroyers and four transports had also been lost in the Solomons area since the landing. The weakened Allied navy could no longer get enough ships into the area to insure the Marines the supplies, ammunition and air and sea cover that they sorely needed.

Aside from the job he was faced with, Halsey felt badly at being ordered to relieve Ghormley, his old friend who had played football with him at Annapolis. The good and well-earned reputations of naval officers could be lost in one battle in those days. Considering the almost impossible job with which he was faced and the tools he had to do it with, Admiral Ghormley had done well, but he had not done well enough. Admiral Nimitz decided that the situation called for a more aggressive commander, and Halsey was such a man.

At least the men in the fleet thought so. In the crowded quarters aboard the *Argonne*, flagship for Advance Headquarters, it seemed that Halsey had barely stepped aboard ship before the word went around: "Halsey's taking over!" and the faces of dungaree-clad sailors lighted up. "Now we'll get somewhere!" was the way the word went. Only one man among them all said, quite honestly, "I don't like serving under Halsey. He scares me." He had served under Halsey before, as far back as the *Saratoga* days, and no doubt he knew that things would not be easy.

Among these men were survivors of the sunken ships

from up north. Here in the harbor at Nouméa only a few days before, the cruiser *Boise* had tied up alongside the *Argonne* with more than 100 dead still in her hold. They had been killed when a Japanese shell breached her number-one turret and exploded a powder magazine.

On Guadalcanal the reaction was even stronger. Battle-weary, malaria-ridden Marines whooped for joy. Pounded night and day by Japanese ships and planes, they had been asking, "Where is the Navy?"

As far as the men in the South Pacific Forces were concerned, Nimitz had chosen wisely. It was Admiral Arleigh (31-Knot) Burke who said: "The great captain must be able to project his personality so that his entire command feel they know him and follow him as an individual. The larger the command, the more flamboyant and theatrical his personality must be, to project the greater distance. We find examples of the truth of this in comparing Jeb Stuart and Jackson with Longstreet and Hill: Halsey with Spruance; Patton with Bradley."

To the men who worked closely with Halsey and knew him well, he hardly seemed a "flamboyant" man. The nickname "Bull," soon to be fastened on him, did not fit him. To anyone who knew him well enough to call him by his first name he was always "Bill."

Yet on a larger scale and to those who knew him less well, perhaps he could be called flamboyant. There was the determined, bulldog face, soon to be staring out from the pages of every newspaper and magazine in America. There was the courage and the will to fight, for he was, first of all, a fighting man. There were, above all, the colorful and pungent phrases which he spoke. He never hesitated to speak out upon any matter in his field, in no uncertain terms, and probably, as he himself admitted, sometimes he spoke when he should have kept silent.

At any rate, the Halsey legend grew, always accenting and often exaggerating the more colorful aspects of his personality. Stories about him, sometimes true and sometimes not, all added to a picture of Halsey as a born leader and fighter.

But at the moment Bill Halsey was not worried about his public image—if, indeed, he ever was. The lifeline to Australia must be held, with very little to hold it. He had to make decisions, and fast ones. His first one—where to put a second and badly needed airstrip on Guadalcanal—turned out to be a wrong one because he lacked knowledge of the terrain. He determined never to make such a decision again without that necessary knowledge.

It seemed as if both Japanese and American forces speeded up the fighting after that. The former were still pouring in supplies and men to their forces on Guadalcanal and putting together a powerful fleet to the northward. Halsey assembled everything he could lay hands on for his Third Fleet, and when the time was ripe, sent word to his commanders: ATTACK REPEAT ATTACK, a phrase that was to become almost synonymous with the name of Halsey.

The Battle of Santa Cruz that followed, only eight days after Halsey took command, was no victory for the badly outnumbered American forces, for they lost the carrier *Hornet*. However, two Japanese carriers were damaged, and they lost many more planes in combat than did the Americans. Meanwhile, Halsey had promised the Marines everything he could get to them, and was keeping his promise. Aided by Army reinforcements, they fought back fierce Japanese attacks that the latter had thought would regain the island of Guadalcanal. This gained more precious time while damaged American ships were repaired and a few more ships sent on their way from the Atlantic Fleet, including the new battleship *Indiana*.

As soon after the Battle of Santa Cruz as possible, Halsey answered the Marines' question of "Where is the Navy?" by going to Guadalcanal himself. The commander of an area of this size and importance was hardly expected to go into the midst of the fighting, but Halsey was determined to learn the situation at first hand. His staff also hoped that the men in the front lines would see him in person. They did, but since he was wearing just about the same uniform as a Marine private, most did not recognize him. When the staff begged him to wave or make some gesture so he would be recognized, he refused.

"It smells of exhibitionism," he said. "The devil with it!"*

Nevertheless, he toured the front lines and learned just what the Marines and the Army were facing on Guadalcanal. He took time for a quick trip to the neighboring island of Tulagi, where the PT boats and most of the small craft had their base. There, to the surprise, flustration and delight of the young skipper, he climbed aboard sub-chaser *PC* 477. He wanted to congratulate the entire ship's company for having sunk two Japanese midget submarines the night before.

He was also forced to give a press conference, a thing at which he had not had much practice, and gave his blunt recipe for victory: "Kill Japs, kill Japs, kill more Japs!" Then he spent a night on the island while the Japanese lobbed shells in his direction—too frightened, he said, to get any sleep although we have only his own modest word for that. Certainly he had sound reason to be frightened, for a Navy doctor talking to him was wounded by shellfire, and did not regain consciousness until he had landed in the hospital at Efate, 700 miles away.

Back aboard the *Argonne* the following day Halsey found that Intelligence reports indicated the Japanese were going to try again, with a fleet far larger than anything Halsey could muster. This time the enemy intended to put enough troops ashore on Guadalcanal so that they would be certain to recapture the island. They planned to bomb the island from the air on November 11, blast it from the sea on November 12, attack with carrier planes on the next day, and land several thousand troops that night. Furthermore, a large part of Halsey's inferior fleet was already committed to delivering the support he had promised General Vandegrift—was, in fact, on the way now, escorting transports and cargo vessels to Guadalcanal.

Somehow the transports and cargo vessels were largely unloaded before the Japanese attacked, and the cruisers and destroyers went out to meet the enemy fleet, which included two battleships. In the battle which followed one of the Japanese battleships went down, but American losses were heavy. Rear Admiral "Uncle Dan" Callaghan and most of his staff were killed when a Japanese shell struck the bridge of the *San Francisco*; Rear Admiral Norman Scott, one of Halsey's oldest friends, was killed soon after on the cruiser *Atlanta*. But for the moment Guadalcanal had been saved, and Vandegrift sent this dispatch to Halsey:

TO SCOTT, CALLAGHAN, AND THEIR MEN GOES OUR GREAT- EST HOMAGE X WITH MAGNIFICENT COURAGE AGAINST SEEMINGLY HOPELESS ODDS, THEY DROVE BACK THE FIRST HOSTILE STROKE AND MADE SUCCESS POSSIBLE X TO THEM THE MEN OF GUADALCANAL LIFT THEIR BATTERED HELMETS IN DEEPEST ADMIRATION.*

The Japanese had retired, but they were coming back, and now Halsey had to make a risky decision. There were not enough cruisers and destroyers left undamaged to continue the battle. Two battleships were on the way up, under the command of Rear Admiral Willis A. Lee, but the narrow waters around Guadalcanal were poorly suited to maneuvering large ships, particularly in darkness. Nevertheless, Halsey ordered them in.

After the Naval Battle of Guadalcanal, Admiral Nimitz said of Halsey: "He has that rare combination of intellectual capacity and military audacity, and can calculate to a cat's whisker the risk involved."*

The battleships could not quite get there in time to save Guadalcanal from another pounding, but the little PT boats so harassed the enemy as to cause him to with- draw before the job was done. Then Army, Marine and

Navy planes went to work on the transports, sinking six of them and destroying the other four on the beach. Few of the Japanese reinforcements ever got to Guadalcanal.

Then, on the night of November 14–15, Lee and his battleships got into the fight, sinking the remaining Japanese battleship.

This was truly an American victory, and another turning point in the war. Had the Japanese won this four-day naval battle, the American troops on Guadalcanal would have been trapped and forced to surrender. Then the Japanese would have had an open road to Australia and New Zealand. Instead, never again did large Japanese forces attempt to reinforce Guadalcanal. The United States and her Allies were definitely on the offensive from this moment on.

Messages of congratulation poured in to Halsey from President Roosevelt, Secretary of the Navy Knox, Admiral King, Admiral Nimitz. Three days after the battle, he was promoted to full admiral, breaking a long-standing Navy rule against having more than four admirals on active duty at one time. There were no four-star pins to be found in Nouméa, so a metalworker aboard a repair ship cut out a pair for him. He handed his old three-star pins to his base commander.

"Send one of these to Mrs. Scott and the other to Mrs. Callaghan," he said. "Tell them it was their husbands' bravery that got me my new ones."*

In December Major General Alexander M. "Sandy" Patch and his America Division relieved the battle-weary, malaria-ridden Marines on Guadalcanal, and the latter went off to Australia for a well-deserved leave.

On February 8, 1943, General Patch advised Halsey that organized resistance had ceased. Halsey sent this message:

WHEN I SENT A PATCH TO ACT AS TAILOR FOR GUADAL-CANAL I DID NOT EXPECT HIM TO REMOVE THE ENEMY'S PANTS AND SEW IT ON SO QUICKLY X THANKS AND CON-GRATULATIONS.

After the war Halsey said: "If anybody had asked me what sort of shoulder patch we felt was appropriate for the South Pacific Force in late 1942 and early 1943, I'd have told him without hesitation, 'a frayed shoelace—fastened with a rusty nail.'"

But the shoelace and the nail had held.

13. MOVING NORTH

I T WAS still a long way to Tokyo, and there were other problems for the Commander South Pacific Forces, problems that could not be solved by his famous slogan, ATTACK REPEAT ATTACK. In the crowded quarters aboard the *Argonne* there was not room for his growing staff to function properly, so he moved it ashore.

From the start, Halsey placed emphasis on the principle of unity of command. He insisted that each task force commander should have full authority over all components of his force, regardless of service or nationality. He told all his subordinate commanders:

"Gentlemen, we are the South Pacific Fighting Force.

I don't want anybody even to be thinking in terms of Army, Navy, or Marines. Every man must understand this, and every man *will* understand it, if I have to take off his uniform and issue coveralls with 'South Pacific Fighting Force' printed on the seat of his pants."*

He never did do quite that, but he ordered all Navy men and Marines in the area to leave off their neckties. It was not just a waste of time and loss of comfort; the important reason was that the Army did not wear them, and he felt that similarity of uniform would make for better teamwork.

Although Halsey was no great stickler for spit and polish, where the pride and reputation of the Navy or efficiency of operations were concerned he could be very firm. On one occasion he sent the following stinging rebuke to the commander of an escort division whose ships were in Nouméa Harbor:

On 7 March a number of the crew of the U.S.S. ———— and the U.S.S. ———— were ashore on liberty at the port at which headquarters is located. I personally observed that many of them were slovenly dressed, their uniforms were not clean and they did not conduct themselves in a military manner. It was necessary to censure some of them for their conduct.

Their appearance and their conduct reflects discredit on our Naval service, and raises doubt as to the efficiency of the ships in question.

From some naval officers, a thorough dressing-down would have been forthcoming upon another occasion. Two sailors were walking down the narrow sidewalk outside Headquarters when the Admiral himself approached. One saluted him, but the other was so wrapped up in what he was saying that he did not even see Halsey until too late. Halsey said nothing; he grinned, returned the salute, and walked on. Apparently he thought that one missing salute to him reflected no discredit on the naval service.

The move ashore had taken place early in December of 1942. On New Year's Eve war correspondents in Nouméa asked Halsey to give them an interview and make a few predictions for 1943. He did so, and stirred up something of a hornet's nest. For one thing, he declared that the Allies now had the initiative and that the end of 1943 would see them in Tokyo. Furthermore, he gave his own blunt opinion of the Japanese and said some rather indelicate things about Emperor Hirohito and Premier Tojo.

The latter statement troubled State Department officials in Washington, who felt that an American admiral should not make such insulting remarks about the leaders of another nation, even an enemy in wartime. The prediction about the early end of the war, according to Halsey, brought from production leaders in America "a bellow that I could hear in Nouméa."* They were afraid that it would cause a letdown in war production. Draft officials also complained. Halsey was accused of recklessness and even drunkenness.

A few days later he flew down to New Zealand to look over American personnel and equipment there, and also because he wished to pay his respects to an Allied government which had repeatedly asked him to go down for a visit. Immediately upon his arrival,

Prime Minister Peter Fraser asked him to report his prediction. His reason was that the people of New Zealand were still afraid of a breakthrough and were demanding that their own divisions be brought back from Africa where they were badly needed to fight the forces of Germany and Italy. Fraser felt that his government could not long withstand such pressure without a reassuring statement from Halsey. Among other things, the Admiral told the press there: "We have 363 days left to fulfill my prediction and we are going to do it."

To New Zealanders such statements did not seem bombastic. The newspapers there spoke of Halsey's "unassuming manner and quiet speech." They wrote that "in all his answers he spoke in a level and deliberate voice, at the same time revealing the confidence which has inspired his men in all the actions fought against the Japanese in this area. No one could listen to him without being convinced that in Admiral Halsey the South Pacific has the perfect leader."

In any case, Halsey at this time did not speak off the top of his head. He knew very well that the Allied forces could not possibly be in Tokyo by the end of 1943, but he also knew that his own men were tired and low in morale and needed to feel some of the confidence in eventual victory that he felt. He had something else in mind, too, according to a statement made by Captain Harold Stassen, later his flag secretary, to the New York *Times*. Stassen said:

We had very little Navy afloat. Australia was very much concerned. The Japanese Navy was still strong. It was a pretty gloomy situation. Halsey knew that if the Jap Navy had attacked our force, it was doubtful if our fleet, even with its magnificent fighting spirit, could hold the line. So he made his bold assertive statement both to mislead the Japs and to cheer up our force. It worked. The Japanese didn't attack for six months. Instead they tried to find out what in the world Admiral Halsey had that led him to make that statement.

Nevertheless, the statement did a great deal to build up the myth, at least in America, of Halsey as a swaggering, loud-mouthed hater of Japs, a salty sailor in the heroic mold. Some men, among them Admiral King, felt that this was not good, that he was too valuable a man, both for American morale and American victory, to present this false image. They felt that his occasional tendency to speak out before he thought of the results, which he himself admitted, made him inept in relationships with the press.

For some time Captain Miles Browning had served as his chief of staff. A good fighting officer, he was an irascible man and the terror of every sailor who served under him. In dealing with the press he was of little help to Halsey. But the Admiral remained sturdily loyal to the men who served under him, as long as he felt they were doing their job, and he had no desire to have Browning replaced. In fact, he had tried hard, but without success, to get the Navy to promote him to rear admiral.

In July 1943, Admiral King relieved Browning. As his replacement, he took Captain Robert Carney from a happy berth as captain of the cruiser *Denver*.

Carney was another good fighting man in whom Halsey had the greatest confidence, and also a man who could handle relations with the press smoothly. The results pleased both King and Halsey. Some time later, when Rear Admiral Carney told King he wanted to get back into battle action, he got a quick answer.

"You'll be Halsey's chief of staff," King growled, "as long as Halsey can fight."

And that was until the end of the war.

But if Halsey could not handle the press well, his natural courtesy combined with a directness of speech made it possible for him to get along with almost anyone else. A case in point was General Douglas MacArthur, although the explanation for it is not easy.

As of August 1942, the Joint Chiefs of Staff had marked 159 degrees east longitude as the line between SOPAC and SOWESPAC. East of this line, Halsey held command of all forces—Army, Navy, Marine and New Zealand—subject, of course, to Admiral Nimitz. West of the line General MacArthur held the same authority, subject to no one save General Marshall and the Joint Chiefs of Staff. As the SOPAC forces moved up the Solomons after the capture of Guadalcanal, they would be getting into MacArthur territory. The Joint Chiefs solved this problem by putting all the Solomons area under tactical command of Halsey, though with MacArthur as strategic commander of most of it. Thus, as Halsey put it, he now wore three hats—Nimitz's, MacArthur's and his own.

With plans in mind for the invasion of New Georgia,

where the Japanese had an airfield which menac__
Guadalcanal, it was time for Halsey to make that
long-delayed visit to see his strategic commander in
Australia. He flew over from Nouméa to Brisbane in
April 1943, having requested an appointment.

It is hard to imagine two men more different in every
way, or two more likely to clash. One was Army-born
and bred, and one Navy. MacArthur was dramatic to
the point of melodrama, Halsey blunt and outspoken.
MacArthur was not accustomed to opposition within
his ranks, and in this instance he was Halsey's superior
officer. And Halsey was a man who could be stubborn
even with his superiors.

Yet the two admired and respected each other from
the start. From the moment they met, neither ever
spoke of the other in public except to praise him. In
addition, Halsey himself said that MacArthur, as his
superior officer, never once forced his decisions upon
the Admiral.

There were arguments, of course, although not at
this first meeting when MacArthur accepted Halsey's
plan for the New Georgia landings. A very serious
argument did occur upon a later occasion that could
easily have ruptured a weaker relationship. It had to do
with the setting up of a certain base in which Mac-
Arthur felt the Navy would be taking over his properly
designated authority. He asked each of his own staff
members present if this were not true, and each assured
him that it was. Then he turned to Halsey.

"What about it, Bill?" he asked. "Am I right?"
Halsey did not hestitate. "General," he answered,

"I think you are putting your prestige above the good of the country."

MacArthur looked as if he had been struck in the face. He got up and paced the floor, a habit of his during such discussions. Finally he said, "That is a very serious charge. No one has ever suggested such a thing of me before. It can't possibly be true."

But Halsey did not retract his words. The talk continued. Suddenly MacArthur smiled and said, "Bill, you are right."

Late in June the landings on New Georgia began. It proved to be a costly operation in ships, men and time. Beginning with Guadalcanal, it had taken nearly a year to get one-tenth of the way to Tokyo. And there were still more islands in the Solomons—and beyond that the Japanese stronghold at Rabaul in New Britain before the Allied forces would be really on their way. It was time for a new tactic, and at that point "leap-frogging" began in the South Pacific. Before this the advance had been island by island; now some of the tougher ones would be bypassed and the Japanese garrisons left "to wither on the vine," for lack of reinforcements and supplies.

Kolombangara was the first to be bypassed. Vella Lavella, which had the needed room for an airfield, was taken instead. This tactic had already been tried successfully in retaking some of the islands in the Aleutians which had been captured by the Japanese. Because of this, according to historians, in July 1943 Admiral Nimitz suggested to Halsey that Kolombangara be bypassed. Halsey's own recollection was that he never discussed this matter with Nimitz, but believed it was suggested to him by one of his staff. In any case, it was no doubt in the mind of more than one man by that time, and it worked. After the war General Tojo, wartime Prime Minister of Japan, gave it as one of the important reasons for Allied victory.

14. GOOD-BYE TO SOPAC

THE NEXT LEAPFROG was to Bougainville, northernmost island of any size in the Solomons group. Rabaul was the long-range objective. Already heavy bombers could reach it from both New Guinea and the lower Solomons, but protecting fighter planes could not. Airfields on Bougainville, only 210 miles from Rabaul, would solve that problem.

Nouméa now was too far from the front lines. Halsey moved his advance headquarters up to Guadalcanal, nearly 1,000 miles closer. By this time they had something to work with—though by no means everything they needed—and they could plan for a sound job. Halsey did not pretend to understand the workings of the Japanese mind, but he had an Intelligence officer who knew them well. Commander "Mike" Cheek, part American Indian, a quiet-voiced man who looked more like a schoolteacher than a naval officer, had spent a great deal of his life in the Pacific. If anyone could outguess the Japanese, Cheek could.

The plan that COMSOPAC worked out made it appear they were interested in almost anything but Bougainville. Landings were made in the Treasury Islands and Choiseul, both below Bougainville. The former could provide a base for motor torpedo boats and other small craft, but the Choiseul landing was purely an attempt to confuse the Japanese. Then, on November 1, 1943, the main landing force fought its way ashore at Cape Torokina on Bougainville.

The great danger here was that the forces of the South Pacific were moving up within close range of a heavy concentration of Japanese ships and planes at Rabaul. Both could blast the landing and supply ships apart before they had completed the job. The transport force, under the command of Rear Admiral Wilkinson, was as ready for this as possible, with new means worked out by which they could unload quickly and get away.

So, as it turned out, was Rear Admiral "Tip" Merrill with his light cruisers and destroyers of Task Force 39. When the Japanese came down with bigger ships and heavier guns the following night, TF 39 turned them back with greater losses than the American forces had taken. The Navy did not lose a single ship, though some were damaged, and the task force went on a few hours later, with some help from Army, Navy, Marine and New Zealand planes, to fight off a Japanese air strike of more than 100 planes.

Thus far the Bougainville landing was a success. It looked as if the fighting spirit instilled into the SOPAC forces by Admiral Halsey with his ATTACK REPEAT ATTACK tactics was paying off. But the worst danger still had to be faced.

Admiral Koga, now Commander-in-Chief, Japanese Combined Fleet, had his headquarters at Truk in the Caroline Islands to the north of Rabaul. As soon as he learned of the landings on Bougainville, he decided to send reinforcements to Rabaul. On November 4 an American plane sighted nineteen ships, including six heavy cruisers, off the Admiralties and headed south.

Things looked bad for Halsey's forces. The Japanese could refuel at Rabaul, then run down to Bougainville the next night and sink the American transports and bombard the Marines ashore. Nor could Tip Merrill's forces stop them. Aside from the fact they already were battle-weary, they did not have a single heavy cruiser. There remained, in fact, not one in the Third Fleet, for Nimitz had had to take all for the forthcoming landing on the Gilberts in the Central Pacific.

Halsey's operations staff went to work and came up with an answer. Rear Admiral Frederick Sherman's Task Force 38 contained two carriers—the *Saratoga* and the light carrier *Princeton*—now fueling south of Guadalcanal. It would be possible for them to make a fast run northward and strike the Japanese ships before they left Rabaul. Yet it would be a desperation measure to risk the carriers that close to the enemy's stronghold. Nevertheless, the staff wrote out a dispatch ordering the strike, and took it to Halsey in his Quonset hut.

He looked it over and his face sagged. His son Bill was Aviation Supply Officer aboard the *Saratoga* and might be lost with the ship. He had met a similar crisis three months before with characteristic forthrightness.

At that time Bill's plane had been reported missing on a flight from Nouméa back to the *Saratoga* at Efate. When they dared break the news to Halsey, who had been down with flu for two days, his operations officer, Captain H. Raymond Thurber, told him what had been done in the way of a search. Rear Admiral Carney suggested additional searches.

"We will not divert a single combat plane from Guadalcanal or anywhere else," Halsey said. "You can use only the planes that are available here for normal passenger travel."

Two days later young Bill and the rest of the crew turned up, unharmed, on an island near Efate.

No, he had no intention of protecting his son more than any other man in his command. As far as that was concerned, the *Saratoga* might well survive the attack. It was the flyers themselves he was thinking of. To strike Rabaul, packed as it was with enemy ships, planes, and antiaircraft guns, would be suicidal. Halsey was convinced that the carrier air groups would be cut to pieces, that hardly a man would come back.

On the other hand, the success of the whole Bougainville operation depended upon stopping those Japanese cruisers. If they were not stopped, the men on Bougainville would be wiped out. In either case, he would be sending a great many men out to die.

"There's no other way?" he asked.

"None, sir."

"Let 'er go!" he said.

Then the Commander South Pacific put his head in his hands and cried.

But the weather was with the flyers that day. It gave them cloud cover against Japanese "snooper" planes. It gave them some cover even over Rabaul. No Japanese cruisers were sunk, but several were damaged, one so badly that it took five months to repair her. Sherman had sent in all his ninety-seven planes, and all but ten came back. The two carriers got away without damage, and the Japanese searchers never found them.

That was enough for Admiral Koga. He called his heavy cruisers back to Truk, and did not send them back to those waters again. In addition, Admiral Nimitz was able to spare a few more carriers for another raid on Rabaul six days later. This one caused Koga to withdraw his remaining carrier planes to Truk. He replaced them with planes from the Marshalls, which was a great help to the American Central Pacific operation.

Despite Halsey's fears, the raid had more than paid off. It had proved that carriers, properly trained in antiaircraft warfare, could successfully move in close on a strong land base. It saved the Bougainville operation and aided the one in the Central Pacific. Happily, Halsey radioed to Sherman:

IT IS REAL MUSIC TO ME AND OPENS THE STOPS FOR A FUNERAL DIRGE FOR TOJO'S RABAUL.

This did not mark the end of the South Pacific offensive, but it was the beginning of the end. Bougainville was eventually secured. In December, orders sent Halsey to Pearl Harbor for a conference with Nimitz, and thence to Washington to talk with Admiral King. Fan and young Bill met him in San Francisco. It was the first time he had seen his wife in sixteen months. It was also the first time that some of his staff members discovered there was one person in the world who could tell him to "shut up" and make it stick. They were delighted.

In Washington, Halsey was awarded a Gold Star in place of a second Distinguished Service Medal. There also, he convinced King that the two Japanese strongholds, Rabaul and Kavieng, could now be bypassed as not worth the effort to capture. His forces would take Green Island and Emirau, which commanded their approaches; MacArthur would take the Admiralty Islands to the north.

They accomplished these objectives in the next few months. At least 50,000 Japanese were sealed into New Britain and New Ireland, and 30,000 more into Bougainville and Choiseul. Land, sea and air came under Allied control. In May 1944, King and Nimitz informed Halsey that he would soon be relieved as COMSOPAC, now getting to be a rear area, and go to sea as COMTHIRD FLEET. He took a final swing around the area. In New Zealand, the Prime Minister informed Halsey that the King had made the Admiral an Honorary Knight Commander of the Order of the British Empire.

His staff started addressing him as "Sir Butch."

On June 15 he turned over his command to Vice Admiral John Newton. The next day he took off for Pearl Harbor. Troops lined the way to the fleet landing in Nouméa. Their cheers and the bands and the flags made his eyes moist. He never saw Nouméa again.

15. THE "DIRTY TRICKS" DEPARTMENT

U P TO NOW the war in the Pacific had been a three-pronged affair, with MacArthur working north from Australia and Halsey from New Caledonia, while the forces of the Central Pacific worked out of Pearl Harbor in a general westerly direction. The latter, a Fifth Fleet, Army and Marine operation under the command of Admiral Raymond Spruance, had moved into the Marshall and Gilbert islands and would soon be invading the Marianas, including Saipan, Tinian and Guam. Thus all three forces were gradually converging, making so many strategic commands no longer necessary.

Under the circumstances, Nimitz felt that he could combine the units of the Third and Fifth fleets into one, giving the Allies a striking force more powerful than anything the Japanese could muster. The losses the latter had taken could not be replaced as quickly as those of the U.S. Navy. At the same time, Halsey and Spruance would continue as commanders of their respective fleets. That is, when Halsey took command it would be called the Third Fleet, and under Spruance the Fifth. As Halsey said, it was a matter of changing the drivers and keeping the horses.

This had more than one advantage. After an operation the commanding officer could retire with his staff to headquarters and plan the next operation he would command, while his alternate took over. Meanwhile, they would have discussed with each other what they had learned that might be of value. The striking power of the "Third Fleet," and on the next operation of the "Fifth Fleet," it was hoped, would give the Japanese the impression they were confronted with two great forces instead of one. In addition, the difference in methods employed by these two commanders was enough in itself to keep the enemy guessing as to just what would happen next.

And they were quite different men. Spruance was a brilliant commander, as he had proved at Midway and since that time. Whether or not as brilliant, Halsey had a capacity for thinking in a straight line that spotted possible errors and danger points in every battle plan brought before him. It seemed to amount to intuition. Spruance was meticulous, with an eye for details. Halsey hated details and paper work; he preferred to leave these matters to his staff, with important problems threshed out in conference. Spruance was not as well known to the public at home as was Halsey, since he spurned publicity and avoided newspapermen. Halsey certainly did not seek publicity, but with his forthright statements and his colorful phrases he could not avoid it. Spruance did not have the color and warmth that seemed to emanate from Halsey. So he did not inspire quite the emotion felt by the men who served under Halsey. But certainly no one who served under Spruance doubted that he was a good man to follow. If he ever erred, it was on the side of caution; if Halsey ever erred, it was on the side of aggressiveness. But neither was prone to error.

They added up to an excellent pair of alternate fleet commanders, and both deserve their share of glory. As General Holland M. ("Howlin' Mad") Smith of the Marines was later to say, "What did Nimitz have to worry about? He had Halsey and Spruance, two of the greatest admirals in the world." Which is pretty fair praise from the man who worried only about his beloved Marines and always felt that the Navy was giving them the short end of the stick.

Upon his relief at Nouméa, Halsey and the senior officers of his staff flew directly to Pearl Harbor, where they settled down at once to planning the next Third Fleet operation. This called for occupation of the western Carolines, north of New Guniea and east of the Philippines. The relations between Halsey and his staff were excellent, for the admiration and affection were mutual. He had messed with them at Nouméa and continued to do so in his present command, yet they never felt ill at ease in his presence.

"When I was a junior officer," Admiral Carney recalls, "and had to mess or dine with officers of flag rank, I felt like a young squirt who had better not be heard and shouldn't even to seen. It wasn't that way with Halsey."

Halsey welcomed and encouraged suggestions even from green ensigns and lieutenants junior grade, and he never objected to a man arguing for his opinion. "You could pound on his desk and swear a blue streak to make your point," Carney says, "and it was fine with Halsey. Once he'd heard enough and made up his own mind, though, then that was it. He wouldn't say a word; he'd just lift one finger, and you knew it was time to shut up."

It took such an atmosphere for Halsey's pride and joy, his "Dirty Tricks Department," to flourish. It had been operating even during the Guadalcanal compaign, but now—with more time to plan ahead and with increasing Allied strength—it could really get rolling.

Probably most of the members of Halsey's staff got into the act at one time or another, but basically the department consisted of Mick Carney, Rollo Wilson (operations), "Ham" Dow (communications), Douglas Moulton (air operations), Harold Stassen (flag secretary), and John Lawrence (air combat information). Their main intention was to keep the Japanese guessing, thus tending to keep them on the defensive, and they had a fine time doing it. They even went so far, upon occasion, as to launch an air strike upon a Japanese position which had no strategic value for the Allies, just to catch the Japanese off base and cause them to shift their defenses.

Such tactics did work. The Japanese did not show as much imagination in their planning. If a system worked once, they were inclined to keep trying it over and over. If something threw them off schedule in the early stages of an operation, they seemed to lack the ability to change their plan to fit the new situation.

Not so the Dirty Tricks Department. It could do a quick shift at any time. Now its members had the opportunity to come up with their best ideas and the time to argue them with each other and with Halsey.

There was plenty of difference of opinion about the Third Fleet's next operation, and on various levels. The original plan called for occupying three islands in the Palau group—Peleliu, Angaur and Babelthuap—as well as the island of Yap and Ulithi atoll. Halsey opposed the general plan; he thought Ulithi should be taken because it would make a good fleet anchorage, but he believed occupying the other islands would be too costly a job for the airfields and anchorages that might be gained. He preferred speeding up the proposed landing in the Philippines.

Halsey was in part overruled by his superiors, Nimitz and King, but they did allow him to drop Babelthuap from the operation. As far as Peleliu was concerned, he was right in that it proved a costly operation for the Marines

Halsey and his staff put to sea on August 24, in his flagship, the fast new battleship *New Jersey*. He did not have much else, for Spruance had been using most of the fleet in the seizure of the Marianas and the Battle of the Philippine Sea. A few days later, with Spruance's operation completed, somewhere in mid-ocean the Fifth Fleet vanished and the Third Fleet took its place. Halsey was in business again.

The heart of the fleet was TF 38 (under Spruance, TF 58). That was Vice Admiral Marc A. (Pete) Mitscher's Fast Carrier Task Force. Halsey could not actually rendezvous with this most important part of his fleet of more than 500 ships for two weeks, and Mitscher did not wait for the meeting. Having finished with the bombing of Iwo Jima, he stood south and hammered the Palaus for three days while one of his task groups hit Yap. The next two days he struck at Mindanao, the southernmost of the large Philippine islands. He had planned further strikes there, but found that MacArthur's Fifth Air Force had already done a flattening job.

The next day Halsey caught up with the task force and rode across on a fancy chair, the most modern equivalent of a breeches buoy, to the *Lexington,* Mitscher's flagship, to talk with him. When Mitscher told him of the situation at Mindanao, Halsey decided to switch his next air strikes to the central Philippines. These would hit the last of the air bases that could cause trouble to the landings in the Palaus.

They might also prove helpful in clearing the way for MacArthur. The latter, with the aid of his Seventh Fleet Amphibious Force, commanded by Rear Admiral Daniel Barbey ("Uncle Dan the Amphibious Man"), had already reached the top of New Guinea, and in two and a half months expected to be landing in the Philippines.

The strikes began on September 12, so close in that the mountains of Samar could be seen from the ships. In two days the task force flew 2,400 sorties. Air Combat Intelligence reported to Halsey that his men had shot down 173 planes, destroyed 305 more on the ground, sunk 59 ships, probably sunk another 58, and also caused tremendous damage to installations. This had been done with a loss of only nine American planes and ten men!

Studies after the war show that the Japanese losses were not that high, but they were high enough to justify Halsey's exuberant dispatch to all the carriers:

TO MY GROUP OF STARS: I AM BOOKING YOU TO APPEAR BEFORE THE BEST AUDIENCE IN THE ASIATIC THEATER BECAUSE OF THE BRILLIANT PERFORMANCE JUST TURNED IN.

What Halsey had in mind as "the best audience" was Manila, where more enemy planes were concentrated than anywhere else in the Philippines. His reasoning was sound. He had just dealt a hard blow to Japanese air power and had met only weak defenses in the central Philippines. Why not try out the hornets' nest itself?

Perhaps it was time to do more than that. Why not recommend that MacArthur shift the planned invasion of Mindanao north to Leyte, and do it earlier than the previously set date of November 15?

He talked it over with his staff. They studied their Intelligance data and combat reports, figured out how many forces were available from Nimitz and MacArthur. Their answer was "Yes."

Halsey sat down in a corner of the bridge and thought it over. It was not his business to make such recommendations. CINCPAC had plenty of good men on his staff who planned operations. So did Admiral King and the rest of the Joint Chiefs of Staff, and the Combined (Allied) Chiefs of Staff as well. It was not easy to switch operations in the middle of things, and it might cause problems all the way up the line—even in the European operation, which always had top priority. Halsey's superiors might easily be annoyed at his interference.

On the other hand, he was on the scene and better able to judge the situation. He thought his idea would save thousands of lives, and it might throw the Japanese off balance and shorten the war considerably.

He sent for Admiral Carney and Captain Stassen. "I'm going to stick my neck out," he said. "Send an urgent dispatch to CINCPAC. . . ."*

The dispatch recommended that seizure of Yap and the Palaus be abandoned, that the ground forces to be used in those operations be put at MacArthur's disposal. It further recommended that an invasion of Leyte be undertaken at the earliest possible date, which would mean abandoning a landing on the southern island of Mindanao.

There was certainly no sign of annoyance from Admiral Nimitz. He answered promptly that the Palaus operation should be continued, since Rear Admiral Theodore S. Wilkinson was already embarking his amphibious forces for the job, but he would give fresh study to Yap. Furthermore, he was passing on Halsey's suggestions regarding the Philippines to MacArthur and Admiral King. A change in operations as great as this required not only MacArthur's agreement, but that of the Joint Chiefs of Staff.

The suggestion could not have come at a better

time. The Joint Chiefs were meeting at that moment in Quebec with the British Chiefs of Staff, President Roosevelt, Prime Minister Churchill, and the Canadian prime minister. Within two days they had word from MacArthur that he was willing to land on Leyte on October 20, two months ahead of schedule. Having, as General Marshall said, "the utmost confidence in General MacArthur, Admiral Nimitz, and Admiral Halsey," they made their decision quickly. Within ninety minutes they had sent messages to Nimitz and MacArthur: Drop the intermediate landings except for Peleliu, and make the Leyte landing in a joint operation on October 20.

If Halsey was "sticking his neck out," he certainly had chosen a good time to do it. President Roosevelt later spoke of the result as "a change which hastened the liberation of the Philippines and the final day of victory—a change which saved lives which would have been expended in the capture of islands which are now neutralized far behind our lines."

Possibly it shortened the war by at least two months; certainly it saved the lives of many Americans held prisoner in the Philippines.

The Peleliu, Angaur and Ulithi landings were made in September, and these were taken quickly except for Peleliu. It took a month and many lives to secure that rocky island.

With the landings secured, Halsey headed his fleet in the direction of Manila. He and his staff had promised themselves an attack on the Philippine capital next. It would be the first since the last Americans had been driven from the islands more than two years before. It was an important objective, since they expected to find heavy concentrations of Japanese planes and shipping in that area.

In spite of its importance, the night before the strike Halsey did something which would hardly be expected of a tough admiral in command of a fleet in wartime, but was quite typical of Bill Halsey. There were a number of Filipino stewards who waited on table for the officers of his staff. He called them all in and pointed out the targets in Manila.

"I want you to know what we're going to do," he told them, "because many of you have relatives in Manila. All of us pray that none of them are injured."

"Those are Japanese installations there, sir?" asked Chief Steward Benedicto Tulao.

"Yes."

"Bomb them!" Tulao said.*

They hit the Japanese four times the next day, destroying or damaging hundreds of planes and sinking or damaging many ships. Clark and Nichols fields were bombed out, and the harbor at Manila was littered with wrecks. The Third Fleet lost fifteen planes and a dozen men, but not a single American ship was touched, although the carriers had launched their planes within forty miles of the coast.

They had to wait two days until the weather cleared and they had had time to fuel, then struck again at Coron Bay, on the western rim of the Philippines where the remaining Japanese ships had fled for safety.

There they sunk and damaged tankers, transports, cargo ships, destroyers, destroyer escorts, and small craft, and destroyed more planes. Halsey promptly sent out a dispatch to his forces:

THE RECENT EXCEPTIONAL PERFORMANCE YIELDED GRATIFYING GATE RECEIPTS, AND ALTHOUGH THE CAPACITY AUDIENCE HISSED VERY LOUDLY, LITTLE WAS THROWN AT THE PLAYERS X AS LONG AS THE AUDIENCE HAS A SPOT TO HISS IN, WE WILL STAY ON THE ROAD.

They did, however, take time out for a brief rest and rearming, refueling and reprovisioning before taking to the road again. This time they went farther north, to begin "running interference" for MacArthur's upcoming landing on Leyte. Having smashed most of the Japanese air strength in the Philippines, they now struck Formosa and the Ryukyu Islands, from which Japanese air reinforcements must come.

This was another successful series of strikes which took place between October 9 and 13, with more than 500 Japanese planes destroyed and at least 40 ships and small craft sunk. Again, American losses in planes were light, with no ships damaged.

Their luck did not quite hold throughout the last day. On Friday, October 13, they started to retire from the Formosa area at six o'clock in the evening. Shortly thereafter a torpedo hit the heavy cruiser *Canberra* and left her dead in the water.

Halsey looked at his chart. The *Canberra* was 90 miles from Formosa, 300 from Aparri Field on Luzon, 400 from Naha Field on Okinawa—and 1,300 from the nearest American base, Ulithi. As Halsey later said: "We were squarely in the Jap dragon's jaws, and the dragon knew it."*

The easy answer, perhaps the sensible one, was to abandon the *Canberra* and sink her, then get safely out of enemy waters with the rest of the fleet. Towing her back to Ulithi would mean a running fight for 1,300 miles, against everything the Japanese could send down. Halsey's decision, quite typically, was to fight it out.

It was indeed a running fight all the way. Before the Japanese planes could come down, Halsey's carrier planes struck at Luzon and Formosa. The heavy cruiser *Wichita* took the *Canberra* in tow, at a speed of four knots, at which speed it would take over thirteen days to reach Ulithi.

Nevertheless, a few Japanese got through. Nearly 100 planes were shot down, but later that night one managed to put a torpedo into the heavy cruiser *Houston*. Now there were two cripples, and the whole task group was under constant attack.

By this time even Halsey was worried. The crippled cruisers were a drag on the entire fleet. In six days, the Third Fleet was committed to support MacArthur's landing on Leyte. Maybe it would be better even now to sink the cripples and get out.

Perhaps it was Radio Tokyo which decided the issue. With the second torpedoing, Tokyo announced that their brave flyers had all but annihilated the Third Fleet and that the Japanese fleet was speeding down from the north to finish the job. Night fighting, with its gun flashes and flaming planes, is a confusing thing at best, and probably the Japanese pilots thought they really had sunk several ships instead of damaging two.

Or perhaps the decision resulted from Halsey's having indoctrinated every member of his staff with his own aggressive thinking. When he himself inclined toward abandoning the crippled ships, Mick Carney and his operations officer, Rollo Wilson, talked him out of it. Here is our chance, they said. Since the enemy thinks he has just about finished us off, "why not hide our real strength, lure him into attacking the task group around the cripples, in the supposition that these are the remnants, and then move in and blow him out of the water!"*

Halsey agreed. The group around the cripples was named "the Bait Division," and its commander told to keep the air busy with "distress" signals. Two of the task groups moved off to the east, where they should not be discovered but would be ready to swoop in to the attack; the other two struck at Luzon again. And Halsey sent a dispatch to Nimitz:

THE THIRD FLEET'S SUNKEN AND DAMAGED SHIPS HAVE BEEN SALVAGED AND ARE RETIRING AT HIGH SPEED TOWARD THE ENEMY.

Admiral Nimitz was happy to pass on this message to the American press, and the newspapers made it famous.

The trick almost worked. Japanese battleships and cruisers were sighted steaming out from Formosa and the China coast, headed in the direction of the Third Fleet. Then, apparently, a Japanese patrol plane sighted the two task groups in ambush to the eastward of the crippled ships. The plane was shot down at once, but the pilot must already have sent out the alarm. The next time any Japanese ships were sighted by American submarines, they had turned around and were heading back for their own territory.

But the crippled cruisers made it safely to their base at Ulithi, and were repaired to fight again. Even before they arrived, planes from Task Force 38 were once more striking the Philippines in support of General MacArthur's landing on Leyte. And very soon, the Navy was going to have need of all the ships it could muster.

16. THE BATTLE FOR LEYTE GULF

THE PLAN for the invasion of Leyte called for a dual command. The forces of General MacArthur, Supreme Allied Commander Southwest Pacific Area, included the Sixth Army, the Australian forces, and the Seventh Fleet—the latter under Vice Admiral Thomas C. Kinkaid, which itself included some Australian ships.

Some of Halsey's Third Fleet was "borrowed" for the operation, including the Third Fleet Amphibious Force under Vice Admiral Wilkinson. Nevertheless, the bulk of the Third Fleet remained under the separate command of Admiral Nimitz and, under him, of Halsey. This seemed a sound idea at the time, for MacArthur, Nimitz and Halsey had been cooperating throughout the war.

Here, however, the situation was a little different, for their vast forces had at last come together across the broad Pacific—to meet, so to speak, in a combined operation in which neither Nimitz nor MacArthur was in supreme command.

MacArthur's landing on Leyte took place on schedule. There is a difference of opinion as to whether or not having naval forces under two commands had an ill effect upon what would happen soon in the Battle for Leyte Gulf. Admiral Halsey felt that it did. In any case, he was soon to suffer harsher criticism than he had ever had to weather.

For the moment the landings at Leyte and the off-shore islands went well, without great opposition. There was no sign of the Japanese fleet. The fact was that the Japanese had believed their own claims of the destruction of most of the Third Fleet. They thought that, as a result, the invasion of the Philippines would be at least temporarily abandoned. When they discovered their mistake, their ships got moving, coming down in three columns upon the islands. The delay cost them such chance as they had to destroy the transports and supply ships at the time of the landings, but they could still be a threat to the troops ashore.

Having furnished the necessary gunfire and air support for the landings, the Third and Seventh fleets prepared to meet the enemy at sea. What followed, from October 23 to 25, was the greatest naval battle of all time, although actually there were four separate engagements. A total of 282 ships were in the battle, 216 of them American, 2 Australian, and the remaining 64 Japanese.

The battle began when the U.S. submarines *Darter* and *Dace*, patrolling the Palawan Passage west of the

Philippines, spotted a Japanese force of battleships, cruisers and destroyers coming up from North Borneo. This was Vice Admiral Kurita's so-called Center Force. The two submarines sank two heavy cruisers and knocked a third out of the war. Equally important, they sent word to Halsey of what was coming his way.

With this word and other spottings, Halsey and Kinkaid were now aware, on October 23, that three Japanese naval forces were moving in. These were Kurita's ships, and the van and the rear of the Southern Force, under Vice Admirals Nishimura and Shima respectively. The Japanese plan was for Kurita's Center Force to sail through San Bernardino Strait, north of Samar and Leyte, while Nishimura and Shima came out through Surigao Strait just south of Leyte. They would then swoop down upon the Allied amphibious forces and fire support ships, from both north and south, and annihilate them. A fourth force, the Northern Force under Vice Admiral Ozawa, had not yet been discovered. This one had a different job to do under the Japanese plan, and it was the one that would later get Halsey in trouble.

Of Halsey's Task Force 38, commanded by Vice Admiral Mitscher, three of the four task groups were available: TGs 38.2, 38.3 and 38.4, under Rear Admirals Gerald Bogan, Frederick Sherman and Ralph Davison. Task Group 38.1, commanded by Vice Admiral John "Slew" McCain, steamed on its way to Ulithi to refuel, replenish supplies, and get a well-earned breather. It was not destined to get that breather.

At daybreak on October 24 the three fast carrier groups launched search planes which spotted Kurita's

Center Force in the Sibuyan Sea, bound for San Bernardino Strait to the eastward. The strait had been mined by the Japanese, with the channels known only to them, so it would have been unwise for the battleships of Third Fleet to sail through for a surface battle. Attack by the carrier planes was the answer.

Halsey sent word to McCain to turn back and fuel at sea, ordered the other three groups to move into position to attack Kurita in the Sibuyan Sea. That day their planes flew 259 sorties. They sank the battleship *Musashi,* crippled a heavy cruiser, and damaged other ships. They believed that they had done even more damage, including sinking the cruiser. Here they were wrong. At any rate, they spotted Kurita retiring to the westward that afternoon, so it appeared that he had had enough. Actually, he intended only to get out of range of Third Fleet air attacks temporarily until such time, he hoped, as Japanese land-based air had counterattacked.

This was the first of the four actions, called the Battle of the Sibuyan Sea.

The van of the Japanese Southern Force (Nishimura) was sighted by Third Fleet planes on the morning of the twenty-fourth. In the afternoon Admiral Kinkaid, Com 7th Fleet, ordered Rear Admiral Jesse Oldendorf, who commanded the fire support ships at Leyte Gulf, to get ready to meet the enemy. Oldendorf had a sizable fleet—six old battleships, eight cruisers, four destroyer divisions, and thirty-nine PT boats. He judged that the Japanese would be coming up through Surigao Strait, only fifteen miles wide at the top, and he certainly got ready for them.

The enemy was coming up in a single line of battle, which gave Oldendorf a chance to use the classic naval maneuver that had been used for 300 years, and could probably never be used again. It is known quite aptly as "crossing the T." To put it simply, you steam across the enemy column at right angles to him, with your ships all thus able to bring all guns to bear, and fire a broadside as each ship crosses. The enemy, in return, can only satisfactorily bring the forward guns on his leading ships to bear on you.

In practice, Oldendorf's plan was a little more complicated than that, and it was beautifully conceived and beautifully executed. The PT boats attacked first with torpedoes, then the destroyers with more torpedoes. After that the cruisers took over, and the battleships.

Nishimura's force was practically wiped out. He lost his two battleships, his cruiser, and all but one of his four destroyers. Admiral Shima, coming up a little later with his part of the Southern Force, lost one light cruiser and quickly decided it was time to retire "temporarily." He got out with no further losses. American losses consisted of only 39 men killed and 114 wounded.

This was the Battle of Surigao Strait, which took place throughout the night of the twenty-fourth and twenty-fifth of October.

In spite of this crushing defeat, the Japanese were not yet through. Kurita's Center Force was coming back, through San Bernardino Strait, still strong, with four battleships, eight cruisers, and several destroyers. Oldendorf's battleships had expended most of the ammunition for their heavy guns, and could not rearm in time to face the Japanese. Halsey's Third Fleet was already out at sea.

At 6:47 on the morning of October 25, a pilot spotted Kurita's force off Samar. There was nothing left to stand up to him but Rear Admiral Thomas Sprague's Task Group 77.4, made up of sixteen "baby flattops"—escort carriers—and their supporting destroyers and destroyer escorts!

How did this happen? The answer has been the subject of a great many heated arguments and will probably be the object of study of naval historians for some time to come.

The Third Fleet, of course, had not been idle, having struck earlier at Kurita's force, and also fought off a violent attack from Japanese planes based on Luzon, which succeeded in bombing the light carrier *Princeton* so badly that she had to be sunk. When search planes spotted Nishimura's Southern Force coming up, it seemed apparent to Halsey that the Japanese Combined Fleet was committed to an all-out effort. The only thing that made it not quite certain was that thus far no carriers had been spotted.

Then, on the afternoon of the twenty-fourth, planes of Admiral Sherman's task group, farthest north of the three, spotted them east of Cape Engaño, the northeastern tip of Luzon, and sent the word to Halsey: 3 CARRIERS 2 LIGHT CRUISERS 3 DESTROYERS. As a sighting an hour later showed, there were actually six carriers, two of them converted battleships, but that only made the bait more desirable. This was what Halsey had been waiting for.

He was aware that Kurita's force had turned back toward San Bernardino Strait, and was therefore a possible threat to the Leyte landing forces. With that in mind, the day before he had sent out to his task group commanders a dispatch setting up a plan for a possible Task Force 34 under command of Vice Admiral Willis Lee. This would include four of the fast new battleships, along with cruisers and destroyers. It was to be activated only if he thought there would be a surface engagement with Kurita. But Admiral Kinkaid's communications picked up the message and took it to mean that the task force had already been set up. This caused later confusion.

Now Halsey had to make a decision. He could hold his entire fleet at San Bernardino Strait and wait for the Northern Force to strike him, but that seemed unsound. The planes of the Japanese carriers could shuttle back and forth from their ships to the fields on Luzon, and that might be disastrous. He could hold back Task Force 34, mainly the battleships, to guard San Bernardino Strait and hit the Japanese Northern Force with his carriers. This he felt unwise, because he could only assume with the knowledge he had that the enemy had a good number of both shore-based and carrier planes, and could very seriously damage the fleet if he split it up.

The other alternative was to take his whole fleet north and strike the Japanese Northern Force.

Halsey walked into flag plot, put his finger on the

chart where the Northern Force had been spotted 300 miles away, and turned to his chief of staff.

"Here's where we're going," he said. "Mick, start them north."*

Rear Admiral Carney sent out the necessary dispatches to the three task groups to join as they headed north, and for McCain to join them as soon as possible. To Kinkaid Halsey advised:

CENTRAL FORCE HEAVILY DAMAGED ACCORDING TO STRIKE REPORTS X AM PROCEEDING NORTH WITH 3 GROUPS TO ATTACK CARRIER FORCE AT DAWN.

At midnight night fighters from carrier *Independence* were sent northward to search and Task Force 38 proceeded at course and speed designed to meet the enemy head on. Halsey's plan was to launch the planes for attack at dawn, then bring in his fast battleships, commanded by Admiral Lee, to finish off the Japanese fleet with shells from the big guns.

At 6:30 the first strike took off and at 8:50 the planes reported one carrier sunk and other ships badly damaged. They also reported the Japanese course and speed. Meanwhile Halsey had increased his speed to twenty-five knots. He rubbed his hands in anticipation. If the enemy held his present course and speed, he would be in range of Halsey's guns before noon. What the carriers had left, those guns would blast out of the water. Halsey thought he was about to realize the dream of every naval officer worth his salt—a surface action. In two wars, he had not yet had the opportunity to command a fleet slugging it out in sight of the enemy.

Meanwhile, however, he had received an urgent dispatch from Admiral Kinkaid: ENEMY FORCE SIGHTED IN SURIGAO STRAIT X QUESTION IS TF 34 GUARDING SAN BERNARDINO STRAIT. Halsey did not receive this dispatch until 6:48 that morning, although it had been sent two and a half hours before. This kind of delay in communications, plus a mishandled dispatch, was to prove a feature of this troublesome day.

Halsey realized now that Kinkaid had intercepted his preparatory dispatch of the day before, although it was not addressed to him. He answered: NEGATIVE X IT IS WITH OUR CARRIERS NOW ENGAGING ENEMY CARRIERS.

He was not seriously alarmed by Kinkaid's dispatch, because at 8:02 he received a second one: ENEMY VESSELS RETIRING SURIGAO STRAIT X OUR LIGHT FORCES IN PURSUIT. Nor was he seriously alarmed twenty minutes later when he received a third dispatch from Kinkaid: CTU 77.4.3 [Sprague] REPORTS ENEMY BATTLESHIPS AND CRUISER 15 MILES ASTERN HIS UNIT AND FIRING ON HIM. Since Nishimura's Southern Force was already in retirement, that would leave Oldendorf's battleships free to move up to San Bernardino Strait and help the carriers. What puzzled Halsey was why air searches by Kinkaid's forces had not spotted Kurita before he got so close.

Eight minutes later a fourth dispatch came from Com 7th Fleet: FAST BATTLESHIPS ARE URGENTLY NEEDED IMMEDIATELY AT LEYTE GULF.

This one surprised Halsey. As he understood his operations order, which will be quoted later, his primary job was not to protect the Seventh Fleet. His job was offensive, to strike with the Third Fleet. Right now he was doing just this. He was speeding north to intercept a force which, he believed, gravely threatened not only Kinkaid and himself but the whole strategy of the Pacific war. Nevertheless he messaged McCain: STRIKE ENEMY [KURITA] VICINITY 11-20 NORTH 127-00 EAST AT BEST POSSIBLE SPEED, and notified Kinkaid that he had done so.

Half an hour later a fifth dispatch came from Kinkaid: our CVES [escort carriers] BEING AT-TACKED BY 4 BATTLESHIPS 8 CRUISERS PLUS OTHERS X REQUEST LEE COVER LEYTE AT TOP SPEED X REQUEST FAST CARRIERS MAKE IMMEDIATE STRIKE.

Halsey was beginning to get annoyed with Kinkaid. He had already ordered McCain to strike. At this stage he did not propose to yank Lee and his big ships out of the battle line. What was the matter with Oldendorf's battleships, anyway?

The answer came a few minutes later, at 9:22, in a sixth dispatch from Kinkaid:

ABOUT 0700 CTU 77.4.3 REPORTED UNDER FIRE FROM ENEMY BATTLESHIPS AND CRUISERS IN [position] X EVI-DENTLY CAME THROUGH SAN BERNARDINO STRAIT DURING THE NIGHT X REQUEST IMMEDIATE AIR STRIKE X ALSO RE-QUEST SUPPORT FROM HEAVY SHIPS X MY OBBS [old battle-ships] LOW IN AMMUNITION.

Halsey was amazed. Low in ammunition! How could that be? What he did not know was that the old battle-ships had been loaded for the invasion of Yap, which never took place, and that therefore they carried a high percentage of bombardment shells, but a low percentage of the armor-piercing shells needed to fight big ships. Most of the latter had been used up in the Battle of Surigao Strait.

And why, Halsey wondered, hadn't Kinkaid let him know this before? He looked at the dispatch, and then he knew. Each such dispatch carries the date and time it was sent. Thus 251224 would mean that it was sent at 12:24 on the twenty-fifth. This one showed that it had been sent an hour and fifty-seven minutes before Halsey received it! Furthermore, checking back on the other dispatches, he realized that this one, received as the sixth, was actually the third one sent out by Kinkaid, soon after he informed Halsey that the escort carriers were under attack! Halsey did not learn until later the reason for this strange delay.

Immediately he answered: I AM STILL ENGAGING ENEMY CARRIERS X MCCAIN WITH 5 CARRIERS 4 HEAVY CRUISERS HAS BEEN ORDERED ASSIST YOU IMMEDIATELY. He also gave his own position, to show Kinkaid that it was now impossible for the fast battleships to reach the latter in time.

Almost at the same time, at ten o'clock, two more dispatches came in, the first from Kinkaid: WHERE IS LEE X SEND LEE. It had been sent "clear," rather than in code, in spite of the fact that the Japanese would probably intercept it. This was a measure of Kinkaid's desperation.

The second dispatch came from CINCPAC, and as Halsey received it, it read: WHERE IS TASK FORCE 34 X THE WORLD WONDERS.

Halsey blew up. He threw his cap on the deck and shouted something that caused Mick Carney to grab his arm and cry: "Stop it! What's the matter with you? Pull yourself together!"*

Halsey was so furious he could not even answer. How could Chester Nimitz have sent him such an insulting message?

Of course, Nimitz had not. All coded dispatches were sent with "padding" at the beginning and end, usually nonsense phrases designed to confuse the Japanese if they tried to break the code. The message, as actually received by Third Fleet Communications, read: TURKEY TROTS TO WATER GG X WHERE IS REPEAT WHERE IS TASK FORCE 34 RR THE WORLD WONDERS.

Here were two mistakes compounded. First, the communicator at Pearl Harbor had used padding at the end that could make sense with the message, which he was not supposed to do. Second, the communicator at Halsey's end had taken out the padding at the beginning but not that at the end, because he thought it did belong to the message. Those two letters "RR" should have shown him where the true message ended, but this time they did not.

Still in a rage, Halsey gave up his hope of a big surface action. At 11:15, having had to reshuffle the task force and allow the destroyers to refuel, he changed course from due north to due south. Two of the carrier groups went on to the north to continue their attacks, but Halsey and Lee's battleships and the third task group went south. And at that time, as he said bitterly, the Japanese carriers had been only forty-two miles from the muzzles of his sixteen-inch guns!

He could not make it back in time to rescue the endangered Seventh Fleet, though planes from Mc-Cain's Task Group 38.1 did arrive in time to harass what was already a fleeing enemy. As it turned out, heroic work on the part of Sprague's little carriers and their supporting destroyers caused Kurita to withdraw when victory was within his grasp. He had sunk two of the carriers, two of the destroyers, and a destroyer escort, but he himself had lost three heavy cruisers. By this time he had learned that the Japanese Southern Force, with which he was supposed to join to put the pincers on Leyte Gulf, had been defeated. He did not think that much could be gained by staying on, and he got out.

The ships Halsey left behind to the north, fighting what was called the Battle off Cape Engaño, did not wipe out all of Ozawa's Northern Force, as Halsey had believed could be done by combined air and surface action, but they did not do badly. Four of the six carriers were sunk, along with some cruisers and destroyers.

Thus the three-day Battle for Leyte Gulf ended as a decisive Allied victory. The truth of Halsey's dispatch to CINCPAC on the night of October 25, THE JAPANESE NAVY HAS BEEN BEATEN AND ROUTED AND BROKEN BY THE THIRD AND SEVENTH FLEETS, was doubted at first by Admiral King, but four days later he radioed Kinkaid and Halsey:

A LARGE PART OF THE ENEMY NAVY HAS BEEN EFFEC-
TUALLY DISPOSED OF FOREVER AND THE REMAINDER FOR
SOME TIME TO COME X ALL OFFICERS AND MEN OF YOUR
FLEETS HAVE THE HEARTIEST ADMIRATION OF ALL HANDS X
WELL DONE.

This certainly proved to be true. American losses were eight major vessels, including two submarines. The Japanese lost twenty-six ships, including three battleships, four carriers, and ten cruisers. Never again would the Japanese fleet be able to put to sea in strength against the Allied Navy.

In spite of this victory, Halsey was criticized at the time for his failure to be on hand when Kurita's force returned and attacked the carrier escorts. His own feeling was that the fault, if any, lay in the divided naval command. Admiral Nimitz did not concur in this, but he did in every respect warmly endorse Halsey's actions. Admiral King did likewise, and stated that if any blame was to be placed, it should be upon Admiral Kinkaid for not instituting air searches that would have spotted Kurita's returning force before it caught the escort carriers. (It might be added here that, in the plan set up for the invasion of Japan on November 1, 1945, which never came off, there was no division of naval command.)

After the war, the criticism of Halsey increased when it was discovered that the Japanese plan had been for Ozawa to lure Halsey away from the main battle, which he succeeded in doing. Actually his carriers had come down with only 116 planes, because the Japanese at the time were too short of trained pilots to man the carriers properly. Most of these planes, after a futile attack upon Sherman's task group, were either shot down or flew on to Luzon and stayed there, so that when the battle was joined Ozawa had only 29 planes. Thus they could not have been the serious threat that Halsey assumed them to be.

When this knowledge came out, a magazine writer wrote a critical article entitled "Bull's Run." Halsey later commented to the effect that he supposed his action would be known forever after as "the Battle of Bull's Run." He continued to assert that, if he had made any mistake, it was in turning back because of Kinkaid's and Nimitz's dispatches.

Was he right in moving north when the landings at Leyte still stood in need of his possible protection? His operations order from Nimitz, approved by the Joint Chiefs of Staff, read that he was "to provide cover for concurrent operations in the Southwest Pacific Area," but also added: "In case opportunity for the destruction of a major portion of the enemy fleet offers or can be created, such destruction will become the primary task." As far as the information available to Halsey at the time was concerned, this opportunity now offered, and he took the orders literally. Getting those Japanese carriers was his primary task.

A commander in the field, faced with battle, must base his decisions upon the information that he has. Halsey did just that. His information was that Kurita's Center Force had been too badly damaged by the air strikes of Task Force 38 to return to the attack. This information proved to be wrong. Until too late he did not know that Oldendorf's battleships were short of armor-piercing ammunition.

Another factor which left him short of exact information was the time lag in communications. It took far too long for Kinkaid's desperate appeals for help to reach him. He did not know the reason for this until after the war. The fact was that radio communications, so vital at such a time when a battle is being fought, were clogged by press dispatches on MacArthur's "return to the Philippines." Such use of High Command circuits had not been authorized by MacArthur, but nonetheless it existed.

Probably a more cautious commander, setting out to catch the Japanese carriers, would have left some of his fast new battleships behind to guard San Bernardino Strait against Kurita's possible return, and in this case he would have been right. Halsey was not a cautious commander, but an aggressive one. That was why he had been made COMSOPAC and commander of the Third Fleet. If he had not been aggressive and willing to take chances, it is doubtful that he could have won the battle for Guadalcanal, on "the frayed shoelace and rusty nail" which were his only resources at the time.

Wrongly or rightly, at the Battle for Leyte Gulf Halsey acted as only a man such as Halsey could have done. When something that looked like a big battle offered, he went out to fight it. It would have been contrary to his nature to do otherwise. He had been a fighting admiral, and he remained one to the end of his career.

17. THE SUICIDE PLANES

THOUGH THE JAPANESE fooled Halsey at Leyte Gulf, it must be said that the shoe was far more often on the other foot. Halsey told the press in September of 1944, "Our Dirty Tricks Department is working overtime." And he noted in his report to Nimitz and King a little later:

"The Japanese are gullible prey to simple deceptive devices; time and again dummy communication traffic, decoy balloons, and movements of minor forces led them to erroneous conclusions and faulty defensive measures. . . ."

Radio deception was now, perhaps, the most often used "dirty trick." This took various forms, but all were designed to keep the enemy constantly harassed and to increase the possibility of a surprise attack upon the Japanese. Thus, when fleet units were in port refueling, rearming or in general taking a breather, a cruiser or destroyer would be sent at high speed to usual strike positions off Formosa or Luzon to fill the air with false radio messages that appeared to be coming from the Third Fleet in preparation for another strike. It worked. Japanese alert orders went out at once. The ship retired before daylight.

During one period in Ulithi all fleet communications traffic was sent via aircraft to Guam every day for transmission. Thus the enemy was unable to learn where the Third Fleet was. Another time, when the Japanese started a night torpedo attack, Halsey's units managed to jam the enemy aircraft circuit. The attack had to be abandoned.

For the three months following the Battle for Leyte Gulf the Third Fleet continued its strikes in support of MacArthur's advance up the Philippines. As far as the job to be done, it was nothing new. But something else was new, and it began almost at once in late October.

After the three-day battle and the long weeks at sea, Task Force 38 was low on planes and its men were exhausted. Since the end of August, around 270 planes had been lost. Operational losses were increasing because of the weariness of the pilots. A flight surgeon on the *Wasp* reported that only 30 of his 131 pilots were fit for further fighting.*

It was time to retire to Ulithi for a breather, but not possible to do so. Kinkaid and MacArthur needed air support. The latter's air force, under Lieutenant General George C. Kenney, could not do the job. There were not enough bombers, and furthermore, Kenney's only serviceable airfield, Taclobán, could not satisfactorily handle all the planes he had.

With the Third Fleet at its lowest strength, the suicide planes swooped down upon the carriers. The Japanese could not have chosen a better time to strike.

Once begun, these suicide attacks continued. The one on November 25 was the worst of all. Halsey saw it from the bridge of the *New Jersey*. The first *kamikaze*, or suicide bomber, dove at the carrier *Hancock*. The ship's gunners brought him down before he struck, but he was directly overhead. A piece of his wing fell on the flight deck and started a fire. Two more planes, both loaded with bombs, crashed into the carrier *Intrepid*, Admiral Bogan's flagship. Two more damaged the *Cabot*.

On this day Task Force 38 was making its last strike in support of Leyte. From where he stood, Halsey began to wonder if it would be its last strike anywhere. An instant after she was hit, the *Intrepid* was wrapped in flames. Blazing gasoline cascaded down her sides, and explosions rocked her. Oily black smoke rose thousands of feet into the air, and Halsey could see nothing but her bow.

Somehow, the *Intrepid* survived, although a number of men were killed and 17 planes destroyed. She had to go back to Pearl Harbor for repairs. Almost a month had passed since the first *kamikaze* attack upon the Third Fleet, and in that time the suicide planes had killed 328 men, destroyed around 90 planes, and temporarily cost the fleet the use of three carriers. When the first attack came, Halsey did not believe this kind of thing could continue. Even the Japanese could not muster enough recruits to keep their "Divine Wind Special Attack Corps," as they called it, really effective.

Now, brooding over what he had seen, he knew he had been wrong. That night, after much coffee and many cigarettes, he dropped in for the nightly meeting of his Dirty Tricks Department. There were worried lines around his eyes and weariness marked his usually rugged face. He was sixty-two years old, living on at most five hours sleep a night, and worrying too much to sleep well. He needed a rest as badly as his pilots did.

Something, he told his staff, was going to have to be done about the suicide planes.

Something was done. Halsey and Admiral McCain, who had relieved Admiral Mitscher as Commander Task Force 38, and their staffs set to work at once on a plan to stop the *kamikazes*. For one thing, they found that the Japanese pilots were trailing the American pilots back to their carriers. This made useless the IFF (a radar device for the automatic Identification of Friend or Foe). Another trick was to come in on a long, fast glide from a high altitude, where the radar would not pick them up. A third system was to skim so close to the water that radar would not spot them until they were too close to be stopped by Combat Air Patrol.

They countered the first method of attack by stationing picket destroyers well out from the task force, and instructing the homing American planes to approach these destroyers on specified compass bearings, then circle them in a specified manner. Planes which did not do this—that is, Japanese planes—stood a good chance of being shot down by the destroyers.

The second method was countered by sending the

CAP higher and farther. The third was handled by patrols that circled at low altitudes.

For long-range defense Halsey established a "constant CAP," which meant keeping a blanket of fighters over all enemy airfields on a twenty-four-hour schedule. The daytime fighters shot down the Japanese when they tried to take off, and the night fighters discouraged them from even trying it.

This called for a great many fighter planes. Instead of thirty-seven fighters per large carrier, the number was increased to seventy-three. This cut down the number of bomber and torpedo planes, but the most powerful new fighter planes—F6Fs and F4Us—could double as bombers when necessary. Halsey asked also for two large carriers with air groups especially trained for night fighting.

It took time to put all these changes into effect, but when even a few of them had been made, successful *kamikaze* attacks on the carriers noticeably lessened. And after the last strike on Leyte the Third Fleet was at last able to head for Ulithi for a few days of much-needed rest. Since leaving Pearl Harbor in August, the *New Jersey* had steamed 36,185 miles, with only ten days in port. Not only were the crewmen and pilots on the carriers exhausted, but Halsey himself was tired in mind, body and nerves. He had only two means of relaxing—reading and deck tennis—the latter only when clear of the combat area. If the deck was too wet after a rain squall to play, he sometimes grabbed a swab and wiped it down himself. As for reading, he said, "Other men may have unwound with the help of noble literature; I used to read *The Police Gazette*."* Actually, according to Admiral Carney, he was a voracious reader, and his reading included a great deal of biography.

In spite of the weariness of himself and his staff, they had barely gotten ashore at Ulithi at the end of November when they began to work out more tricks to fool the Japanese and stop the *kamikazes*. Obviously the use of suicide planes was a desperation measure, and in a way it reflected the seeming inability of the Japanese to plan on a long-range basis.

American pilots, after a reasonable length of time in combat, were sent home to train new pilots. Thus there was always a growing reservoir of well-trained men. The Japanese, on the other hand, tended to keep their good men in the field until they were shot down— perhaps as much because of exhaustion as for any other reason. Thus they were beginning by 1944 to run out of good pilots. But a poor pilot in a rickety plane might occasionally get through to crash on the deck of a carrier as long as he did not mind dying for the Emperor. This was believed to be a glorious death, insuring its reward in the Hereafter.

Even then the *kamikaze* attacks were not highly successful. They sank some ships and damaged several others, and one pilot and one plane seemed a small price to pay for sinking a carrier or even a destroyer. But that was not really the price. Halsey estimated that, once the Navy had perfected its defenses, only about one suicide plane in 100 got through. The rest crashed in the water or were shot down. The real price, then, was 100 pilots and 100 planes per successful attack. At that rate, it seemed that the Japanese would soon be running out of even poor pilots and ramshackle planes.

The plan for the Battle for Leyte Gulf was another example of poor planning or desperation measures. Had the Japanese succeeded in destroying a large part of the Seventh Fleet, including the escort carriers and the battleships, as they hoped to do, what then? They could have wreaked considerable havoc with MacArthur's landing force, but at best only temporarily. Even if Halsey had kept on going north till he caught up with Ozawa, he would have been back at Leyte in less than two days with his vastly superior force. He would have wiped out the Japanese fleet and the invasion of Leyte, slightly delayed, would have gone on.

As interviews after the war showed, the Japanese plan did not even go that far.

MacArthur's invasion of Mindoro Island, just south of the main island of Luzon on which Manila stood, was now scheduled for December 15. The Third Fleet sortied from Ulithi on December 11. Its job was to hold down the Japanese fields on Luzon and so keep the enemy from intercepting the American transports. For three days in a row, the carriers hit with everything they had. Estimates at the time showed that they had destroyed 270 Japanese planes at a cost of 27, as well as sinking 33 ships. Not a single Japanese plane got closer than twenty miles to the ships of the Third Fleet.

Unfortunately, one of the ships sunk off Luzon

was carrying American prisoners of war. The pilots, of course, could not possibly have known this. It was learned afterward only because two of the prisoners managed to swim ashore and were rescued. Much later, the mother of one of the prisoners who had gone down with the ship wrote a bitter letter to Halsey, saying, "Even the detestable Germans occasionally stop and pick up people, whereas you run off and leave them. You ought to be hung as a war criminal!"*

Of course, she did not realize that carrier planes had no way of picking up people in the water. Probably she did not understand that for the ships themselves to go in that close to the waters off Luzon would have been suicidal. Nevertheless, Halsey was miserable. He paced the bridge and brooded. For days he kept referring to the letter.

"Doesn't she realize that these things are bound to happen in a war?" he would say, and he kept asking his staff over and over, "How could our pilots have known?"*

Sometimes, for Halsey, the rewards of victory were bitter.

18. INTO THE CHINA SEA

IN November it had been the *kamikazes*; in December an even greater disaster struck the fleet than the most fanatical Japanese could invent. This was a typhoon, the Far Pacific version of a tropical hurricane. Not all the aggressive strategy that Halsey and his staff had devised in three years of war could cope with this airborne monster. Not, at least, without exact information as to how to escape it, which they did not have in time.

It first began to make its appearance on December 17, 500 miles east of Luzon, when the destroyers were trying to fuel from the bigger ships in preparation for further strikes on Luzon. Fueling at sea, which is done by bringing hoses from one moving ship to another, is a ticklish and dangerous job in the best of weather. But with a wind up to thirty knots and a cross swell it is next to impossible. The destroyer *Spence* was trying to fuel from Halsey's flagship, and as he watched from the flag bridge both her forward and after hoses broke in two. Within the next hour, half a dozen destroyers reported similar trouble, and the wind and sea were increasing.

Halsey ordered fueling stopped and consulted with his staff weather man, who said it appeared that a tropical storm was located about 500 miles to the east. Although it was now moving to the northwest, he thought that it would collide with a cold front soon and swing to the northeast. On the basis of this, Halsey ordered a new rendezvous with the tanker force the next morning, 200 miles northwestward.

But the weather man's estimate, based on all the information he had at the time, proved wrong. An hour later a delayed report came in from an aircraft tender that the storm center was less than 200 miles southeast of the fleet's present position. At that rate, the fueling rendezvous would be right in the path of the storm!

It might have been possible to escape this storm, but such a course would have put the fleet too far from Luzon to make the promised air strike. MacArthur's forces needed that strike. This was war, and chances must be taken. Halsey set up a third rendezvous with the tankers, to the southwest, for seven o'clock the following morning.

By that time, the typhoon had changed course. Its center in time swung within thirty-five miles of the fleet! Once again, fueling had to be stopped and the strike in support of MacArthur canceled. Wind velocity went as high as ninety-three knots, and the barometer was tumbling.

Men were washed overboard and could not be recovered. Planes on a light carrier broke loose on her hangar deck and caught fire. Rudders jammed and ships tossed about in the waves, with all steering control gone and engines dead.

Even the huge battleship *New Jersey*, which had once been hit by a five-inch shell without Halsey even feeling the impact, was tossed about "as if she were a canoe." Seas 70 feet high smashed her from all sides, and the rain and scud were blinding. "At broad noon," Halsey said, "I couldn't even see the bow of my ship 350 feet from the bridge."*

But the destroyers had it worst of all. The modern destroyer is designed to take rough weather. She can roll over a full ninety degrees—that is, to flat out on the water—and still come back. But that is with the weight of normal ballast in her hull to bring her back. These ships were low on fuel, some being down to ten percent of capacity, and there was no weight to bring them back. Water poured down their ventilators and intakes, shorting electric circuits and knocking out their power. With the power went their steering, lights and communications, leaving them voiceless dead hulks in the water.

Three destroyers went down, and with nearly all hands. More men would have been lost, and perhaps the destroyer escort *Tabberer*, had it not been for the courage and remarkable seamanship displayed by her skipper, Lieutenant Commander Henry Plage. With ships around them barely keeping afloat, he maneuvered alongside the sinking destroyer *Hull* and hauled ten of her men aboard.

As an old destroyer skipper, Halsey was impressed with this example of fine shiphandling. He messaged Plage: "Well done for a sturdy performance!"* Later he awarded him the Legion of Merit.

Meanwhile he had inquired into Plage's past experience. Here must be a man who had "cut his teeth on a marlinespike."* Instead, he found that Plage was a Reservist who had never been to sea before, except for a short cruise during his ROTC course at Georgia Tech!

"How," Halsey said, "could any enemy ever defeat a country that can pull boys like that out of its hat?"*

In spite of such men, the typhoon had damaged 21 other ships aside from the 3 destroyers. A total of 790 men were lost and 200 planes wrecked. Since the Battle of Savo Island, the entire Japanese fleet had not been able to cause that much damage without paying for it. The strikes in support of MacArthur had to be abandoned while the fleet limped back to Ulithi to repair the damage done by that storm.

They arrived there the day before Christmas. That afternoon Chester Nimitz, now a five-star fleet admiral, flew in from Pearl Harbor by plane and was piped aboard Halsey's flagship. He brought along a Chirstmas tree, completely decorated.

Nimitz and Halsey now had time to talk over future operations. For some time, Halsey had been wanting to raid the China Sea area. Several Japanese warships were reported stationed along the coast of Indochina. Even more important, that area was supplying oil, rubber, rice, and other things vitally necessary to Japan. After all, in order to get these things Japan had started the war. Halsey felt that a strike aimed at her shore facilities and shipping would cut down her ability to fight. Before the invasion of Leyte he had urged MacArthur to clear Surigao Strait, mined by the Japanese, as soon as possible, so that the Third Fleet could go through.

At the time Admiral King had been dubious about Halsey's plan, and had firmly ordered him to stay out of the China Sea until he had authority from Nimitz to go in. As he said later, "I am afraid that my superiors worried about my judgment in the presence of a juicy target."* Perhaps they did, but in any case he was given the go-ahead this time by Admiral Nimitz. After his next assignment, which was to cover MacArthur's landing at Lingayen Gulf, on the main island of Luzon, on January 9, he could move into the China Sea.

Halsey was jubilant. The day after the Third Fleet sortied from Ulithi, on New Year's Eve, he picked up the speaker of the TBS (Talk Between Ships) and broadcast to all hands:

"This is Blackjack [his code name] himself. Your work so far has been superb. I expect even more. Keep them dying!"*

They hit Formosa on January 3 and 4, in spite of foul weather, then struck the Japanese fields on Luzon on the sixth. Halsey wanted to strike Formosa again the next day, for he never did believe in passive defense. He wanted to hit the opposition at its source, which in this case was Formosa. MacArthur asked him to stand by one day more, however, and he agreed.

Task Force 38 destroyed seventy-five Japanese planes on the ground that day, and also knocked down the only four that managed to take off.

The next day they hit Formosa with everything they had, to prevent enemy air attacks on the landing at Lingayen. And that night, once their planes were back aboard the carriers, they took the course Halsey had been wanting to take for months. They headed into the China Sea. Up to now that had been considered a Japanese preserve and safe hunting ground only for submarines. It was time, Halsey figured, that he made it otherwise.

At one point in their passage through Bashi Channel, they were only eighty miles from the Japanese air base at Koshun on Formosa. They expected attack, but none came. As it turned out, that night the Japanese planes were busy taking their key men out of Manila. Before the next morning, three large transport planes came onto the task force's radar screens, heading from Manila to Formosa. All three were shot down by American night fighters, and one came down close enough to the *New Jersey* so that Halsey could watch it burning brilliantly until it sank.

Immediately, the Japanese radios went hysterical. Those transports held the entire operations section of the Philippine Air Command!

Nevertheless, the Third Fleet was venturing into dangerous territory. The China Sea was almost completely encircled by Japanese airfields, yet the fleet had to try to cross it undetected. If the enemy spotted them, the Japanese ships would run for Singapore into waters so dangerous that even Halsey knew it would be fool-hardy to follow. But if he could creep up and pounce, the whole Japanese supply line from the Asian main-land would be disrupted, and enough shipping might be sunk to shorten the war considerably.

In spite of the difficulties, Plan Gratitude, as it was named, was, in the words of historian Samuel Eliot Morison, "a bold and beautifully handled operation." The two night fighter carriers, which Halsey had asked for and received as a defense against the suicide attacks, went with their screen at the head of the force. These planes would make a predawn search for enemy shipping and pass on the word to the other two task groups following close behind. Behind this mighty armada came the courageous force of tankers, which would be sitting ducks for any *kamikazes* that might get through.

They did not get through. That night three Japanese fighters were shot down by CAP before they could give the alarm. And before dawn the Third Fleet struck.

They did not get the big ships, the *Ise* and *Hyuga*, for they had already gone to Singapore, but they did get at least 2 cruisers, as well as more than 100 planes on the ground and in the air. All told, and in spite of bad weather that hindered later strikes, they sank 47 ships totaling 150,000 tons, and damaged many more. They made a shambles of the Indochinese coast and shattered the Japanese supply route that the latter so sorely needed. In a matter of days control of the South China Sea had changed hands, and the Japanese knew it.

Even better, losses in American planes were very light. Again, no enemy plane was able to get within twenty miles of the Third Fleet itself.

For the time being, the Third Fleet's job was done. On January 26, Spruance relieved Halsey, and it became the Fifth Fleet once again. In five months at sea Halsey's force had destroyed an estimated 7,315 planes, sunk 90 warships and 573 merchant vessels totaling more than a million tons. Halsey sent a typical message to all hands: NO WORDS CAN EXPRESS MY PRIDE. . . . SUPERLATIVELY WELL DONE. Then, for the time being, his job was over and he could go home and see his family again.

He had earned a rest, and he badly needed one. Five months at sea, working from five in the morning until midnight and often longer, had taken their toll. His eyes were getting worse and he found it increasingly difficult even to read. He was tired, dead tired, and a little saddened at leaving his ships and men.

But he could still burst out laughing, as he did while waiting for a plane to take him back to Pearl Harbor and the States. A message from General MacArthur was handed to him. It read: YOUR DEPARTURE FROM THIS THEATER LEAVES A GAP THAT CAN BE FOULED ONLY BY YOUR RETURN.* MacArthur, of course, had said "filled," not "fouled," but the word had been garbled in transmission.

19. JAPANESE WATERS

FOR HALSEY a few months of comparative quiet followed. He was resting at Pearl Harbor when news came that the Army had entered Manila. Later in Washington, with Fan at his side, he received from President Roosevelt a Gold Star in lieu of a third Distinguished Service Medal. It was the last time he would see Roosevelt. Back in Pearl Harbor again in April, he started planning with his staff for future possible operations. He went on to Guam to CINCPAC Advance Headquarters. There Nimitz informed him he would relieve Spruance in about a month. His new flagship would be the *Missouri*, since the *New Jersey* was being overhauled.

In the past two months, the Fifth Fleet had provided gunfire support and air coverage for the bloody but successful assault by the Marines on Iwo Jima, and was now doing the same for the Okinawa landing, a combined Army and Marine operation. Halsey flew on to

Okinawa to confer with Spruance. Then he went back to Pearl, and was there when Germany surrendered.

He hoisted his four-star flag in the *Missouri* on May 18. As he came aboard he told her captain: "This is a significant day. I served in the *Missouri* forty years ago, and here I am back again!"*

Eight days later they were anchored off Okinawa, and at once Halsey began a series of conferences— first aboard ship with Ray Spruance and his staff, and then ashore with Lieutenant General Simon Bolivar Buckner, the big, soft-spoken Kentuckian who commanded the invading forces. Halsey hated paper work; he always maintained that if you wanted something done quickly, a five-minute conversation was far better than a ten-page report. He proved it here by pointing out to Buckner that the radar-warning system ashore, set up to warn of incoming Japanese planes, was not satisfactory. Buckner had not known of this and had it corrected at once.

Conferences and action were both characteristic of Halsey. He was due to relieve Spruance at midnight the following day. A few hours before that, as the *Missouri* stood out to sea, he gave orders to drop a few sixteen-inch shells on the Japanese forces. He wanted them to know he was back.

What troubled Halsey, though, was that he could not attack quite as he wanted to. In this battle the *kamikazes* were at it again. Now they swooped down on the fleet by the hundreds, hitting in particular at the destroyers and destroyer escorts, which stood guard on the picket line to catch them before they struck the ships in the harbor and the troops ashore. In the end Okinawa would cost the Navy 36 vessels sunk, 369 damaged, more than 4,900 sailors killed or missing in action, and more than 4,800 wounded. Normally the soldiers and Marines ashore suffer by far the greatest losses in an amphibious operation, but in this case the Navy's came close.

Because of this, and because of the lack of sufficient airfields on Okinawa, the fleet had been held in what Halsey considered static defense, protecting the ground forces instead of blasting enemy airfields in Japan and Formosa and getting the suicide planes before they started on their way. SOWESPAC planes had been hitting Formosa, but not the airfields, and the same was largely true of the B-29s bombing Japan. Halsey considered this unwise, yet there was little he could do about it at the time.

He did do a bit, however, arranging through General Buckner for setting up more radar stations to take the place of some of the Navy picket ships. He also arranged, with Nimitz's approval, to transfer a Marine air group from the Philippines to Okinawa. This made it possible for one task group to go to Leyte for badly needed rest and repairs, and the others followed in mid-June.

On June 21 organized resistance on Okinawa ended. On July 1 the Third Fleet sortied from Leyte to do the job Halsey had been bursting with impatience to tackle for a long time—to hit Japan where it hurt most, in the homeland itself. They were ready now to take the war home to the Japanese.

On July 10 carrier planes of the fleet hit Tokyo.

There was little antiaircraft fire, and only two Japanese planes came near the carriers. Both were shot down. The American pilots did not even spot many Japanese planes on the ground. The fact was that the Japanese had carefully hidden most of their remaining planes. They were saving them for mass suicide attacks when Allied amphibious forces landed on Kyushu, Japan's most southerly island. This invasion, scheduled for November 1, fortunately never had to be made.

Four days later, in spite of floating mines and the danger of submarines, fourteen ships of the fleet really brought the war home to the Japanese. Rear Admiral John Shafroth, who had relieved Vice Admiral Lee as Commander, Battleship Squadron Two, took three battleships, two cruisers, and nine destroyers so close to shore that any Japanese who cared to look could have seen them. For the first time they bombarded the main island of Japan with naval gunfire, and in broad daylight, blasting the ironworks at Kamaishi.

The next day Rear Admiral Oscar Badger took another bombardment force into the jaws of the enemy, blasting a coal and steel center on Hokkaido, Japan's northern island. This time the American ships were landlocked on three sides, and among them was Halsey's flagship, the *Missouri*. For an hour he watched the big guns pouring in a thousand tons of shells. After the years of waiting it was to him a magnificent spectacle, but he kept glancing nervously at the sky, expecting an air attack at any moment. None came, though the fleet was in plain view for the three-hour approach and the three-hour retirement.

Nonetheless, Halsey remembered it as the longest seven hours in his life. After they were over, he could relax and take his daily constitutional, walking forward from Number One turret up to the bow of the "Mighty Mo" and back again.

It is Navy protocol when an officer of flag rank (commodore or admiral) passes by for enlisted men and junior officers to rise and snap to attention. In the early days of the war, aboard the *Enterprise*, when Halsey was not quite so exalted in rank, it had been convenient for him, on the way to the flag bridge, to pass through a room where members of the plane crews lounged between flights. The first time this happened, a radioman gunner remembers, everyone jumped to attention. Halsey waved them down.

"Boys," he said, "take it easy. Just relax when I come through."

This was not so unusual. Many a courteous admiral, the moment he sees the men starting to rise, will tell them to sit down. They will do so, but they will still rise if he passes by again, believing that the admiral expects them to.

Not Halsey. The next time he walked through the lounging room, the men rose again.

"Blast it," he said, "take it easy! I meant what I said. Don't get up again when I come through."

They didn't.

On this day, as he walked up to the bow of the Big Mo, a group of sailors relaxing on the deck immediately rose. With four stars on his collar, a mighty fleet under his command, and over three years of grueling war behind him, Halsey had not changed. He grinned and said: "At ease, men. None of that stuff on my ship while we're in this area."

Nor, in spite of the responsibilities and the worries of his command, had he changed in other ways. Somehow he found the time, though less often than in peacetime days, to walk among the men and talk to them while they were working. He would ask them how they liked the job they were doing, the ship they were on, the Navy in general. Especially he liked to praise them when praise was due.

"He left you with a feeling," one sailor remembers, "that the job you were doing was worthwhile."

On July 16, while they fueled for further strikes, the fleet was augmented by Task Force 37—four large carriers, a battleship, and several cruisers and destroyers. This was the fast carrier task force of the British Pacific Fleet under the command of Vice Admiral Sir Bernard Rawlings. With the war over in Europe, the British were now able to join their American, Australian, Dutch, and New Zealand Allies in the Pacific.

Vice Admiral Rawlings reported aboard the *Missouri* wearing a trim blue uniform. He found Halsey wearing "a Marine woolen jacket, a blue flannel shirt, green flying trousers, and a long-billed cap like a sword-fisherman's."* Nevertheless, they became friends at once. Halsey, who had been worrying a few minutes before about "how to get on with the British," quickly found that he had no worries.

For the next few weeks the combined fleets ranged

up and down the Japanese coast at will and all but unopposed. They bombed Tokyo and bombarded installations from the sea. They sank everything they could find that was afloat. Finally they even ventured to hit the Kure Naval Base on the Inland Sea, where most of the remaining ships of the Japanese Navy were docked, with bombs, rockets and torpedoes. Admiral "Slew" McCain, now commander of the carrier task force, was opposed to this, but Halsey insisted. After all, Nimitz had ordered the Japanese fleet destroyed, and Halsey intended to destroy it.

By the time they were finished, the Japanese Navy had very nearly ceased to exist. There were left only one damaged battleship, five damaged carriers, and four cruisers, two of them damaged. Only five destroyers were still fully operational, out of an original 177. Hundreds of planes had also been destroyed or damaged.

In spite of typhoons and other bad weather, the strikes continued without further serious delay, except in early August. Nimitz had sent an officer of his staff to the *Missouri* ten days before to brief Halsey on the atomic bomb. On the date that the first bomb fell, Halsey was to keep his own planes at least fifty miles from the target area in southern Japan. By that time he had shifted to more northerly targets because of a request from MacArthur. The General thought that the Japanese had massed several hundred planes up there for an attack on Okinawa. He wanted Halsey's pilots to hunt them down and destroy them. They did—nearly 400 of them. The next day they got a few hundred more.

That was August 10. That night Mick Carney read a radio intercept in the wardroom. It said: "Through the Swiss Government, Japan stated that she is willing to accept Allied surrender ultimatum issued at Potsdam, provided they can keep their Emperor. . . ."*

Halsey and his staff had been expecting this event, and were ready for it. Already plans for an early August retirement had been canceled because if the Japanese actually surrendered, the Third Fleet would be needed. It was the only military unit close enough and with power enough to take over in Japan until MacArthur's occupation forces could arrive. A landing force, composed of a regiment of Marines and four naval battalions, British and American, had been organized. The Third Fleet was ready.

But the war was not over yet.

20. JAPAN SURRENDERS

NOT EVEN at the moment when peace seemed at hand did Halsey lose his hatred of the Japanese. This was the fire that had kept him going throughout the long years of war, and it probably lasted throughout his life. Though he was a man of strong likes and dislikes, the former far outnumbered the latter. But not in the case of the Japanese.

When Mick Carney brought the message to him he is reported to have turned to his chief of staff and said: "Have we got enough fuel to turn around and hit the so-and-sos once more before they quit?"

Even if he did not actually say this, the thought may have entered his mind.

There was, in fact, some reason for him to continue the strikes. Official dispatches indicated final surrender to be probable, but no suggestion had come to Halsey that he stop his attacks. It was certainly not yet clear that Japan had surrendered. The comment in the wardroom of the *Missouri,* according to a staff member, Lieutenant Dana Bergh, USNR, was: "The Japs have surrendered, or something."

On the following day, Halsey ordered the fleet to refuel as planned. Bad weather delayed a strike the next day, and Halsey held a staff meeting to discuss what to do. He did not really want to attack if the enemy had actually surrendered, and he wanted even less to risk the lives of his airmen unnecessarily. The majority of the staff agreed that the honorable course was to cease fire. Admiral Carney, however, argued that they had never trusted the Japanese before, and this was a poor time to start. Finally Halsey signaled McCain: UNLESS THE NIPS BEAT US TO THE PUNCH BY THROWING IN THE SPONGE ATTACK TOKYO AREA TOMORROW.

Then, at one o'clock in the morning on the thirteenth, orders came from CINCPAC to cancel the strike. Halsey passed the word along, adding: SITUATION NOT CLEAR BUT MAY DEVELOP RAPIDLY X MEANWHILE MAINTAIN STRONG DEFENSIVE CAP.

A little later he messaged McCain: IF ENEMY SEARCHES OR SNOOPS I INTEND TO ORDER IMMEDIATE ATTACK.

Moments later a dispatch from Nimitz arrived, canceling his order not to attack. It was now three o'clock in the morning. Halsey messaged the task force: STRIKE AS ORIGINALLY SCHEDULED.

So, as Lieutenant Bergh reported at the time, "the force that Admiral Halsey liked to call the 'Big Blue Team' renewed the attack."

They put more than 400 Japanese planes out of

action that day. Twelve of these were "snoopers" and nine were *kamikazes*. Peace or not, the Japanese were still fighting, but none of their planes got through to the fleet.

The next day the Third Fleet fueled. Early the following morning, August 15, three strikes lined up to go out. The first strike was on its way back and the second on its way out when, at 6:14, a message came through from Nimitz: AIR ATTACK WILL BE SUSPENDED X ACKNOWLEDGE.

A short time later the official word came through. Japan had really surrendered. The war was over.

Halsey recalled that one of his thoughts was, "God be thanked, I'll never have to order another man out to die!"* Then pure joy took over, and he yelled and pounded the shoulders of everybody near him.

After that he ordered the carriers to stow their bombers and torpedo planes on the hangar decks, leaving their fighters on the flight decks and keeping a vigilant Combat Air Patrol in the air. He was taking no chances on the *kamikazes* making a last-minute try. He also had his fighter directors send the CAP pilots the word: "All snoopers will be investigated and shot down, not vindictively, but in a friendly sort of way."

One pilot asked another, "What do they mean, 'not vindictively'?"

"I guess," the other pilot answered, "they mean use only three guns instead of six."

At 11:13 that morning, a large "Well Done" pennant snapped into the air on the *Missouri*. It was accompanied by whistles and sirens from every ship in the force. Halsey and Carney stood on the flag bridge. "How sincerely the Admiral meant 'well done,'" Lieutenant Bergh reported, "was revealed by the soft sparkle in his eyes."

Fortunately, his warning to the CAP pilots did not go unheeded because before the day was over, they, along with the antiaircraft gunners, had been forced to shoot down eight more Japanese planes. These planes were trying either to bomb or to make a suicide dive into ships of the fleet. At the time Halsey assumed that the Japanese pilots were determined to die fighting, but he later discovered that his force had so wrecked the Japanese communications system that their pilots probably had never received word of the surrender.

While the Japanese planes were still being shot down overhead, the Admiral sent a long message to the fleet. Among other things he said:

I have been greatly privileged and honored to have been entrusted with so many active and key combat commands. That fades into insignificance in comparison to the honor of commanding the splendid personnel over whom I have been placed. In the history of our great nation, we have never produced finer, more courageous, or greater fighting men. . . .
Again and again—God bless you and 'Well Done.'

This was not mere speechmaking. He meant every word of it.

The sun went down upon a world at peace, with Admiral Halsey in command of the greatest combined fighting fleet of all history. And in that fleet, the boatswain's mates had already started the sailors to holystoning the gray battle paint down to the white teak-wood decks below and to polishing the brasswork which had been ignored during combat. The sailors quite understandably grumbled. The war was over and they wanted to go home. Why should they be doing this kind of work?

The answer was that of all boatswain's mates in recorded history: It kept the men busy.

In this case, as it happened, it was Halsey himself who had ordered the cleanup. He was thinking of morale as much as appearance. He feared that these men, after over forty days at sea, working long hours and under constant threat of attack, would fall apart at the seams if suddenly left with nothing to do. Probably he was right, although it's doubtful if any of the men agreed with him.

There was still plenty for his hard-working staff to do. On August 28 the Third Fleet, save for most of the carriers, steamed in to Sagami Bay, the entrance to Tokyo Harbor, and dropped anchor. Their guns were still at the ready and their planes overhead, for they were taking no chances. There Japanese officers came aboard and arranged for the surrender of Yokosuka Naval Base. That night the sun seemed to be setting directly into the crater of Mount Fujiyama.

MacArthur had wanted all forces to land at once, with no recovery of Allied prisoners of war until the Army was ready to liberate them. In the latter case, Halsey did not want to wait, for he had already heard tales of inhumanity from two escaped British prisoners who had been picked up along the shore by a picket boat. He ordered Commodore Rodger Simpson to take his rescue task group, including a hospital ship, up to Tokyo and stand by. On the next day Fleet Admiral Nimitz flew in from Guam and boarded the *Missouri*, and Halsey told him what he wanted to do.

"Go ahead," Nimitz said. "General MacArthur will understand."*

Halsey sent word on to Simpson, and immediately rescue parties headed ashore for the various prison camps. By nightfall they had brought out nearly 800 prisoners.

The official landings began on August 30, and on that day MacArthur also flew in from the Philippines. Headquarters of the Third Fleet were established at Yokosuka at 10:45, and Halsey's four-star flag was raised over the station. According to Halsey, Nimitz gave him a thorough bawling out for breaking his flag ashore in the presence of a senior officer (MacArthur) and ordered him to haul it down. Nonetheless, Halsey recalled with a certain boyish glee, it was the first United States admiral's flag to fly over Imperial Japanese territory.

On September 2, 1945, at 9:00 in the morning, the Japanese surrender took place aboard the *Missouri*. A total of 258 Allied warships were anchored in Tokyo Bay, with others outside. Fleet Admiral Nimitz was already aboard, with his five-star flag flying from the aftermast. As soon as MacArthur came aboard, his five-star flag also went up. Commander William Kitchell, long Halsey's flag lieutenant, escorted them to the latter's cabin, with Halsey following just behind.

As he later said, he supposed that some truly histor-

ical words should have been spoken at that moment.
Instead, Halsey said:

"General, will you and Chester have a cup of cof-fee?"

"No thanks, Bill," MacArthur answered. "I'll wait
till afterward."

"So will I, Bill," Nimitz said. "Thanks all the same."*

At 8:56 the Japanese envoys came aboard. Those
from the Foreign Office wore morning coats, silk hats
and striped trousers. The military came in full uniform,
with riding boots. This was in odd contrast to the
Allied officers, who were in plain khaki uniforms, with
shirts open at the neck. An even odder contrast was
Halsey. Most of his compatriots at least wore their
gold-braided caps. He wore his cloth, fore-and-aft
garrison cap.

Once the Japanese had signed the surrender docu-
ments, MacArthur, as Supreme Commander of the
Allied Powers, followed. Nimitz was next, as represen-
tative of the United States. Following him came the
signers for Great Britain, Russia, Australia, Canada,
China, France, the Netherlands, and New Zealand.

At 9:25, at a word from MacArthur, Halsey passed
on a prearranged signal. Moments later 450 planes
from Task Force 38, along with a number of Army
planes, roared mast-high over the *Missouri* and other
ships.

The war was now officially over, 1,364 days from the
day when Pearl Harbor had been struck.

Spruance was to relieve Halsey on September 20,
after which he would sail home to Navy Day celebra-

tions in the States. In the meantime, a minor indiscretion came back to haunt him. The year before, in Washington, he had announced that when the war was over he intended to ride Emperor Hirohito's white horse, and this statement made the headlines. Now, Major General William Chase, commanding the First Cavalry Division, invited Halsey ashore in Tokyo, supposedly for lunch and to inspect his troops. When he got there, the Admiral found a white horse waiting for him.

Halsey had no taste for horseback riding. But as he once wrote to Captain Gene Markey, his former public relations officer, "I have made a monkey out of myself many times, and I will gracefully submit to other people making a monkey out of me if it is necessary."

He rode the white horse.

In October, as Commander Task Force 30, he sailed into San Francisco Bay, his battleship accompanied by other battleships, a cruiser, destroyers and submarines. He had to come in aboard the *South Dakota*, since the *Missouri* was wanted on the East Coast for ceremonies by President Truman, a Missourian.

After a mighty celebration ashore and a speaking tour across the country, his flag was hauled down from the *South Dakota* for the last time. He told the ship's company:

"I am terminating a seagoing career of slightly over forty-five years. This is far from a pleasure, but I deem it necessary for men of my age to step aside so that younger men can take over the greatest Navy in the world. . . .

"You have heard the nation say, 'Well done!' I say it again and again: 'Well done! Well done! Well done!' May you all have happy careers! Godspeed and God bless you!"*

At last Bill Halsey was leaving the Navy that he loved above all else, and the men who had served under him. It hurt.

Or almost leaving it. The Navy was not yet ready to let him go—not quite.

21. SAILOR ASHORE

EVEN BEFORE he left Tokyo Halsey had requested retirement as soon as he was relieved. He
felt that his job in the Navy was done. Both Nimitz and
King had approved his request, but that did not seem
to be enough. When he objected to taking the speaking
tour to sell war bonds, he was promptly awarded a
Gold Star in lieu of a *fourth* Distinguished Service
Medal.

After that, instead of being retired, he was promoted
to fleet admiral, the highest existing rank, and previously held only by King, Nimitz and Leahy. In most
instances five-star admirals and generals are not
allowed to retire; when they are, they are still subject
to recall to active duty.

By now Halsey was sixty-three years old and tired
from the long years of war. Both his hearing and eyesight were bad. He had earned, if anyone had, retirement to a quiet life. But he was a national hero, and

his own aggressive words and actions had made him so. Perhaps he would have found himself unhappy in complete retirement, but he did not get a chance to prove that. The Navy gave him an office in Washington, but he spent no more time there than he found absolutely necessary. After his superior, Fleet Admiral Nimitz, served his tour as Chief of Naval Operations—the Navy's top job—Halsey would have been the logical choice for the position, but he did not want it. Though the Navy always remained his first love, once his seagoing days were over he preferred to be out of the service entirely. He told Mick Carney that he never had lived in Washington and wanted no part of the place.

Fortunately, he did not have to stay in Washington a great deal of the time, for he was constantly being sent around the country and abroad on public relations and goodwill tours. He found the time to visit the Pingry School, his old preparatory school, in Elizabeth, New Jersey, where he met a few of his classmates. He told the boys of the school, "Be anything but mediocre. That is an unforgivable crime."

Perhaps his most notable goodwill trip was to Latin America in 1946. Everywhere he went there, he was joyfully welcomed.

Finally, on March 1, 1947, he was allowed to go on the Retired List of the Navy, but he did not stop working. He joined the boards of two companies in the communications field. He led—unsuccessfully—the campaign for the preservation of the *Enterprise* as a national shrine. He was also called back to his alma mater, the University of Virginia, to take over as chairman of the university's development fund, to raise some $8,800,000. In this he proved more successful.

In spite of all these jobs, Halsey did not neglect other things he considered his duty. He acknowleged all correspondence, all obligations, no matter how trivial. A study of his correspondence makes it appear that just about anyone who had ever served under him, regardless of rank, felt free to write him. Sometimes men wanted a job, sometimes advice, sometimes merely a word from him. He helped when he could; even when he could not, he nevertheless answered the letter.

The records show that even after his supposed retirement the Navy recalled him twelve times to active duty, the last time less than two months before his death. One of these assignments consisted of a month's trip through Australia and New Zealand.

In the summer of 1959 he went to Fishers Island Country Club off the Connecticut coast for rest and relaxation. There, on August 16, he died in his sleep, of a heart attack. He was buried with full military honors in Arlington National Cemetery, beside the graves of his father and mother. The governments and navies of a score of nations paid him homage.

What kind of a man was this bulldog-faced, fighting—some even said blustering—admiral. In 1948, he himself expressed his own philosophy in print:

The best defense is a strong offense. That is a military principle, but its application is wider than war. All problems, personal, national or combat, become smaller if you don't dodge them, but confront them. Touch a thistle timidly and it pricks you; grasp it boldly, and its spines crumble. Carry the battle to the enemy! Lay your ship alongside his!

His life proved that he followed this philosophy. But the words of those who knew him best add considerably more to the picture. At the time of his death, Admiral Carney said that he "engendered a greater affection and loyalty than I have ever seen rendered to any other military leader." A gunner's mate on the *New Jersey* said: "He always respected us enlisted men and never let us down, and we tried never to let him down." Another spoke of him as "one of the most strictly honest human beings I have ever encountered."

A few words spoken by Admiral Carney at the dedication of Halsey Field in San Diego in 1961 sum him up thus:

Tirelessly he kept unrelenting pressure on the enemy, always keeping the enemy guessing as to his intent and next objective, retaining the initiative, never allowing the enemy to get set, achieving surprise after surprise. And so it went through the long months with the Old Man driving and pressing to the very end.

In some curious way his personality was felt and understood down to the lowest rank and rating. They sensed his sympathetic understanding of people, and they responded to his demand for bold and aggressive action.

Quickly it came to be understood that his war motto was "Attack." His tough talk delighted the troops—and amused those who knew him to be a softie who suffered tortures when he ordered his people to desperate tasks.

He sought counsel and wanted it stated fully, frankly,

and honestly; he had no more patience with timidity at the conference table than he did in action. But he made the decisions. He always had the courage to face up to the solitude of command and to make decisions however hard they might be. . . . He had an extraordinary memory, and his instinctive reactions to plans and proposals again and again proved themselves to be wise and sound.

He was skillful, resourceful, and wise in the conduct of war, and his leadership inspired his forces to heroic action —and, when necessary, to sacrifice.

He was a man for his time. And he deserves to be ranked among the great fighting admirals of all time.

INDEX

219

220

The Author

CHANDLER WHIPPLE served under Admiral Halsey throughout the Guadalcanal campaign. Later he saw action off New Guinea and Okinawa, ending his wartime naval service as a public information officer on the staff of Fleet Admiral Nimitz. He has been an editor, a freelance writer, and has published widely on naval and other subjects. Mr. Whipple and his wife now live in an eighteenth century farm house in the Berkshire Hills of Massachusetts.